Praise for:

Making the Right Impression

"This book could be called *What They Didn't Teach You in Dental School*. This book is a must-have for the dentist-turned-business owner—a great resource for any doctor in any phase of your career if you're thinking about an office project of any type. I have known Jason for over twenty years and would turn to no one else for guidance in this field."

—*Nick Morio, DDS, MS*
Private Practice, Morgan and Morio Oral Surgery
Assistant Professor, University of Iowa Hospitals and Clinics

"This book gives the new practitioner and seasoned practitioner alike many pearls of wisdom that are invaluable for making your dental office what it needs to be in this ever-changing and demanding world! Jason has artfully demystified the dental office design and construction process!"

—*Kaaren Vargas, DDS, PhD*
Diplomate, American Board of Pediatric Dentistry
Owner, Corridor Kids Pediatric Dentistry

"When we first met Jason, we were unsure how to proceed given our circumstances. My son had just graduated from dental school, and we were looking to establish a father/son state-of-the-art practice on a very short timeline. Jason and his team were able to convert a challenging space we found into exactly what we envisioned. Now, after three years in our office and having our office featured in a national dental publication, I can say—thanks to Jason—we have achieved our goals."

—*Gary J. Goebel, DDS & Thomas J. Goebel, DDS*
Owners, Goebel Family Dentistry

"As a young practitioner, the idea of forming, designing, and owning my own dental practice seemed insurmountable. Trusting Jason Drewelow to guide me toward this aspiration was the smartest decision I made. As a dental specialist, I recognize the importance of entrusting complicated tasks to those with the highest level of expertise in the field. In working with Jason, I was continuously impressed by his knowledge, experience, and dedication to my vision. Jason Drewelow is truly spectacular, there are not many like him in our industry."

—*Natalie A. Frost DDS, MS*
Diplomate, American Board of Periodontology
Owner, Frost Periodontics & Dental Implants PC
Adjunct Clinical Faculty, Creighton University School of Dentistry &
The University of Nebraska Medical Center College of Dentistry

"Dental schools do a fantastic job in training individuals to be great clinicians; however, they do not provide adequate training dentists to run a successful business or build a practice. This book helps every dentist to be a successful business owner and successfully complete a dental office project. Jason Drewelow is a highly skilled professional in helping dentists and specialists achieve their dream practice.

He helped me with site selection, financing, architecture, and construction. I now have the office I always dreamed of at a very young professional age and now can grow my practice to be extremely successful while continuing to make a long-lasting impact on the lives of my patients."

—*Dave Kujak, DMD, MS*
Owner and CEO, Kujak Orthodontics

"This book is a must-read for any dentist looking to renovate or build a new dental practice. Jason answered all of my questions and concerns about a dental office project. It definitely took the fear out of building a new office and helped me know the best way to move forward."

—*Scott Craven, DDS*
Owner, Excelsior Springs Family Dentistry

"I've had the pleasure of working directly with Jason on two large-scale practice projects and can honestly say there is nobody else I'd rather have in my corner. The experience and knowledge Jason possesses and shares in this book leaves no doubt as to why he is the authority in the field of dental office design, construction, and expansion. This book is a must-read for anyone in the dental profession—regardless of their current situation—thinking about an office project!"

—*Christopher M. Tyler, DDS*
Owner, Tyler, Link and Barnes, DDS

"Jason's book will save any dentist thousands of dollars in design or project consulting fees. It will serve as a guide and will help answer questions you would not know to otherwise ask. Read the book, build your dream office, and I guarantee you will smile!"

—*Mike Scott CEO, Neighborhood Dental Clinics*

"Our multi-doctor office building was one of the first designed and built by Primus Dental, home of Jason Drewelow. It has remained one of the premier facilities in our area. We have since made changes to accommodate growth, and Primus was there to help with the planning and the work. Jason's book reads like a history for our practice and the path we took. If you are considering a remodel or new build, this book is a must-read."

—*Douglas J. Horton, DDS*
Owner, Horton Family Dentistry
Adjunct Professor, University of Iowa College of Dentistry

"We have had the opportunity to work with Jason on multiple projects over the past few years. Initially he helped us design and build the most unusual (octagon-shaped) endodontic office space available. Not only was his team excited for the challenge but Jason was knowledgeable and accessible throughout the entire process. He took what was a daunting task and presented it in an easily digestible format. The result was a unique office designed around a distinctive structure, and it turned out to be a piece of art!

Fast-forward a year later, and we've again relied on Jason and his team to build an entirely different office. We dreamed of building a practice that would accommodate every dental specialty and had no question in our minds that Primus Dental was the only company qualified for the extensive job. Jason's knowledge of the dental field and his ability to visualize what the clinician sees and what the clinician needs is unparalleled. After completing two separate projects with Jason and the Primus team, we are confident that there is no equal in the field. Due to their unique skill and experience with dental office planning, design, and construction, the entire process from start to finish ran smoothly. They considered every last detail so we could focus on patient care. Thank you Jason for your hard work and dedication and for making our dream a beautiful reality."

—*Joe D. Vela, DDS, PhD*
Owner, Endodontic Associates of Iowa
Owner, Dental Specialists of Iowa
Adjunct Faculty, University of Iowa College of Dentistry,
Department of Endodontics

—*Kaci C. Vela, DDS, MS*
Owner, Orthodontic Associates of Iowa
Owner, Dental Specialists of Iowa

"*Making the Right Impression* provides a game plan for dentists to begin to think about the various possibilities that could be open to them and their office—definitely a required read before making any future practice decisions. This book will help you masterfully blend the physical needs of your practice with your individual philosophy of dental care. When the tangible and intangible aspects of your practice come together and meld into a functional office that creates an ideal experience for your patients, then you and your office team will be truly happy and productive campers."

—*John Doering, DDS*
Professor Emeritus, College of Dentistry, University of Iowa

"Jason Drewelow has proven his weight in gold by helping my professional group develop state-of-the-art facilities to practice our specialty skills. Site selection, design, financing, planning, and construction—this book covers every aspect of your project. If you want to learn a seamless and practical approach to completing your dental office project, read what Jason has to say."

—*Dr. Michael Rovner*
Orthodontist and CEO, Central Iowa Orthodontics

Making the Right Impression

The Definitive Guide to Renovating, Expanding,
or Building Your Perfect Dental Practice

Making the Right Impression

The Definitive Guide to Renovating, Expanding, or Building Your Perfect Dental Practice

Jason M. Drewelow

Published by Advantage, Charleston, South Carolina.
Member of Advantage Media Group.

ADVANTAGE is a registered trademark and the Advantage colophon is a trademark of Advantage Media Group, Inc.

Printed in the United States of America.

ISBN: 978-1-59932-697-9
LCCN: 2016933927

Book design by Matthew Morse.

This publication is designed to provide accurate and authoritative information in regard to the subject matter covered. It is sold with the understanding that the publisher is not engaged in rendering legal, accounting, or other professional services. If legal advice or other expert assistance is required, the services of a competent professional person should be sought.

Advantage Media Group is proud to be a part of the Tree Neutral® program. Tree Neutral offsets the number of trees consumed in the production and printing of this book by taking proactive steps such as planting trees in direct proportion to the number of trees used to print books. To learn more about Tree Neutral, please visit **www.treeneutral.com**. To learn more about Advantage's commitment to being a responsible steward of the environment, please visit **www.advantagefamily.com/green**

Advantage Media Group is a publisher of business, self-improvement, and professional development books and online learning. We help entrepreneurs, business leaders, and professionals share their Stories, Passion, and Knowledge to help others Learn & Grow. Do you have a manuscript or book idea that you would like us to consider for publishing? Please visit **advantagefamily.com** or call **1.866.775.1696**.

To my family—Sarah, Caleb, and Javin.
I love you all dearly and am thankful for the journey
we're on together.

Contents

Acknowledgments

Many thanks to...

...KC Dietz, for his incredible expertise in the world of dental office architecture. Few are as skilled at designing dental offices, and even fewer personalities blend knowledge, humility, and humor as his does. It's an honor and an adventure working alongside him.

...Dave Dahler, a great friend whose understanding of financing, practice start-ups, and the overall business of dentistry has proven invaluable to me over the years.

...Bart Woods, for his personal mentoring and coaching, especially in the areas of real estate development and "people skills." His authentic Christian character sets a constant example for our team.

...Ron Stallman, for ongoing guidance in tax matters and all things related to dental accounting.

...Jim Hunter, for insight into the complex world of SBA financing.

…my dad, David Drewelow, for his wisdom and coaching as a kid and even now with life and business. Although I didn't always listen, thanks for loving me and sticking by me!

…the team at Primus Dental, whose tireless work and commitment to excellence has made our organization great.

…my friends Scott Dorrity, Gavin Schramm, Garrett Hufford, and Ryan Lingenfelter for their input and their encouragement with the book, in business, and in life.

…Sheila Buff, publishing editor, Nate Best, editor, and Scott Neville, editorial manager—thanks for your work in sharpening, refining, and shepherding this book.

…and finally, the doctors whom I've had the honor and a privilege to work with and who chose to place their trust in me and the Primus Dental team. We are grateful and humbled to play a part in helping you realize your vision for your practice.

Introduction

Numerous studies over the past fifty years have repeatedly demonstrated that people form impressions within seven to thirty seconds of coming into contact with something. In fact, an in-depth study by Princeton psychologists showed that people form impressions of a stranger in as little time as one-tenth of a second and that longer exposure to that person doesn't significantly alter the initial perception.[1]

But what about the impressions made when they first see your office? Patients form an impression of you and your dental practice within seconds of walking in the door—even while they're still in the parking lot. You want that first impression to tell patients that you're a skilled and caring dentist, just as the skillful way you make a dental impression tells them the same thing.

When patients see a dental office that's run down or beat-up, they often conclude—rightly or wrongly—that the dentist provides sub-

---

1   *Observer* 19, No.7 (July 2006).

standard care. They might think, "If he cares so little about the way his waiting room looks, how much will he care about how my mouth looks? If his waiting room is so old and shabby, what about his dental equipment?"

An attractive, welcoming, up-to-date office is crucial for patient acquisition and retention. At the same time, a successful dental practice needs clinical areas and support spaces in their correct locations in order to maximize the efficiency of the practice, reduce bottlenecks with patient flow, and enhance the well-being of the doctor, staff, and patients.

This book will help dentists look objectively at their offices and decide if it is time to renovate, expand, or build—and if so, how. It will also help dentists considering opening their own practice learn the best way to do so. As general manager of Primus Dental Design & Construction, I work with dentists every day to create custom offices that make them more efficient and more effective at their craft. For any dentist, a crucial item they must be mindful of is an up-to-date and fresh-looking office. Well-kept landscaping, fresh paint, clean carpets, comfortable waiting room furniture—these all tell patients that you're a competent dentist who is current with the latest procedures and technology.

While creating a good patient perception is important for growing a dental practice, at its core a dental office must be laid out correctly, with everything in the right place. The office must be efficient and optimized for the practice of dentistry. It's not enough for an office to just look good on the surface. It has to flow and function well.

In the clinical area, for example, patients want to see comfortable, clean, well-lit, properly equipped operatories. They may decide, after seeing operatories with outdated, patched-up equipment or décor that is old-fashioned or showing its age, that they want to switch to a dentist who pays more attention to the patient experience.

Similarly, the sterilization area for any dental office must be completely up to date with the latest equipment. Here too, a proper setup tells patients that you take infection control very seriously and do everything you can to meet and exceed sterilization standards. At the same time, an efficient and centrally located sterilization area helps with patient throughput and room turns. The faster you can get instruments processed and back into use, the better. As we'll discuss further in chapter 7, the size and location of the sterilization area are central concerns in the planning for a renovation or new office.

Another important area to consider is the check-in/checkout area. When the check-in area is confusing or hard to find or the path to it winds through the seating area, patients may feel the office is cold and unwelcoming, even though the staff is warm and friendly. If the checkout area isn't large enough, patients will stack up there and have to wait to leave the office. They will be annoyed about wasting their time and may decide to look for a dentist whose operations are more streamlined.

I met recently with a doctor who is in exactly that position. His successful, eight-year practice had two years left on its office lease. The big question we needed to answer was *what now?* Renewing his lease and expanding into the space next door was an option, but it might not have been big enough to give him everything he needed to grow his practice. Should he lease a bigger space somewhere else, or should he build his own building because he's tired of paying rent? He could put that money in his pocket instead. Ultimately, when presented with the facts associated with each option, this doctor chose to build a new office when his lease expired—a decision that might have been different given a different set of circumstances.

Each dental office project option has its own set of costs and its own set of pros and cons. We help doctors figure out what works for their individual practices and their individual circumstances and implement the choices they make.

This book will help you take an objective look at your office and your individual practice and decide if it's time to renovate, expand, or build—and if so, what's the most efficient way to move forward.

Chapter 1:

Growing Pains

As your dental practice becomes more successful, you as the owner-dentist have some decisions to make about your office space. In almost every case, an upgraded office can lead to significantly improved collections or a reduction to your stress level caused by facility-related issues. Renovation, expansion, or building all take some of your time and inevitably cause some disruption, but in our extensive experience, the return on the investment of time and money is amply repaid.

Understanding Your Goals and Establishing a Team

When considering what project option is right for you and your practice, the first critical step is surrounding yourself with a team of advisors who understand your personal and professional goals. And in order for your team to know and understand your goals, you first need to have a clear understanding yourself. Working through a series of questions (a process we call Vision Casting) will help you understand the objectives of your project, so you can them relay them to your team.

Ask yourself questions such as:

- What are my goals for the building or leased space?
- How long will my practice likely remain in the current space?
- What are the long-term goals for my practice?
- Is practice expansion (more associates, more chairs, more employees) part of my plan?
- How many chairs/operatories should there be?
- What should the waiting room and patient checkout area look like?
- Do I want to offer additional services, such as in-house specialists?
- What would I want patients to say about the office?
- How do I want to set my practice apart from other practices in the area?
- How do I want to change the mix of procedures and clients (increase hygiene, do more restorative work, see more pediatric patients)?
- Do I want to move into a niche area?
- What do I want my practice to be known for?
- What are my personal preferences for my work space (natural light, high ceilings, noise levels, etc.)?

Understanding your vision is a foundational step for your future and for carrying out a successful project. The answers to these questions impact the entire direction of your project. That's why we suggest starting here because it is an intensely personal decision that reflects your goals and dreams. A dental office project is one of the biggest financial decisions you'll ever make. It is important to get it right.

Once you have an understanding of your vision, you can then relay this information to your project team. A trusted project team can help with a number of things for your project, including further clarifying your goals, conducting negotiations, securing financing, developing architectural plans, and reviewing project options. Depending on the scope and complexity of your project, your team could include the following:

- dental office architect
- dental equipment specialist
- lender
- dental office builder
- technology consultant
- accountant
- attorney
- realtor

It is critical to work with a trusted team that understands dentistry and has specific knowledge in this field. You don't want to spend your time educating your advisors on the ins and outs of dentistry. You need a team who knows what things are important to dentists, from a tax and liability standpoint to a financing and floor plan standpoint. Work with people who have a proven track record in your industry. If you're unsure of someone's relevant experience, ask them. Ask for references or a client list, and talk to people they have worked with in the past. Surrounding yourself with a good team will minimize your stress during the project and help ensure a successful outcome. And while having a good team is critical, it's also important to have someone capable of managing the efforts of the entire team on your behalf. You, as a dentist running your own practice, most likely do not have the time to manage a large team and project. Having a strong team leader to coordinate the efforts of all project team members and serve as your primary point of contact will drastically reduce the amount of time and energy you need to spend on the project as it progresses.

Renovate the Office

A dental office may need to be renovated to upgrade its appearance and modernize the equipment. Owner-dentists must work through a number of decision points to decide what must be changed. Most importantly, they must look at the big picture, not just at the outward appearance of the office. Owner-dentists must review whether their operatories need to be upgraded, if another one should be added, if the lab space and back office space could be improved, and so on. Because we bring years of experience to office renovations, we can also bring up issues you might not think of or know about, such as handicapped accessibility and electrical wiring to support new equipment.

Appearance is the first point to discuss. Some owner-dentists know they need to upgrade the appearance of their office. They still have dark paneling and wallpaper from the 1970s, or they might be a bit more modern and have pine or pickled oak paneling from the 1990s. The need to renovate is obvious. Some who are in newer offices may not realize that the office has started to look a bit worn and that it is time to replace the carpeting in the waiting area and generally brighten things up.

At first, many dentists don't realize that their office has come to look outdated or even shabby. They don't spend a lot of time looking at the offices of other dentists. They're busy practicing dentistry. In fact, they're so busy that they may have no idea how poor an impression their office makes on people. They've been in the same place for years. They're comfortable with it, to the point where they don't really see it anymore. They have a lot of loyal patients who keep coming even though the office isn't as modern as other dentists in town, so the office appearance isn't cutting into their revenues. It's like that blind that fell down in the guest bedroom. You know you should hang it back up when you get a chance, but you never quite get around to it. You walk by it every day for a year, and eventually it's just fine that it's down. After a while, you don't care.

When it comes to the decision to renovate for an improved appearance, many doctors need an objective perspective from someone knowledgeable in such a matter. Look at your office from the point of view of a new patient. Is the office appearance professional and appropriate? Does it seem welcoming? Is the appearance in line with the people you're competing to attract? How does it compare with other dental and medical offices in the area?

A clean, up-to-date reception and seating area helps create a positive impression on both new and existing patients when they visit your office.

These questions help owner-dentists begin to think about the things they like in an office and the things they don't like. Is their waiting room space large enough? Should the seating be replaced? What about the check-in/checkout area? Do patients sometimes pile up there and have to wait to be helped?

Owner-dentists may also need to renovate the clinical spaces of their office. In older offices, the operatories are often small. In many cases, they're not sized appropriately for the way dentistry is performed today. If you have an old, small operatory with newer, larger equipment in it, it's going to be very cramped and hard for you and your staff to work efficiently and comfortably. The doctor may be bumping his chair into the side cabinets, or the assistant may have trouble getting in and out of the room. I've seen situations where if the assistant must leave the room, the doctor has to stop the procedure, stand up, and move out of the way so that the assistant can walk out.

Often the equipment in the operatory is old and out of date. It's so patched up that it breaks down frequently, leading to a lot of down time for the practice. That cascades into a lot of problems as you wait for a service technician to arrive and fix the problem. Then the patient schedule gets backed up, or patients might even need to be canceled and rescheduled. At best, this annoys patients, and at worst, it could lead to losing them forever. Old, worn equipment can have a negative trickle-down effect on the way the practice operates.

Sometimes the goal is to convert the style of the operatories from one form to another. At one time we did a lot of open bay dental offices, where the space was wide open and there were no walls in between the operatories. Often just a small cabinet divided the space between treatment chairs. This style still has value for some types of practices, particularly for orthodontists and pediatric dentists. A lot of general dentists who tried this have said to us in the end, "My patients really prefer more privacy." Sometimes updating the operatories means converting those spaces into actual treatment rooms by building walls and doorways to provide more privacy. Today, it's more common to not have the open bay spaces for general dentists.

Patients don't see the lab space and the back office space, but these areas often need renovation more than any other part of the office. Many times, the lab space or the X-ray space is designed around old equipment that is not used anymore. There might even be a disused darkroom that dates back to when the office was using film-based X-rays. Hardly any dentists still do this anymore, so the renovation can address repurposing that space. This space can be converted into walk-in storage closets, or the area can be recaptured and used in another way for a more clinical space. Some are big enough to become treatment rooms.

Often, older offices have the lab and sterilization area combined into a single space. That's undesirable because it can lead to contamination. Lab work is messy—when you're grinding and polishing, you are generating dust that shouldn't be near sterile instruments. One good reason for doing a renovation is to separate those spaces into their own respective rooms. Another good reason is to create a larger, more centralized sterilization area—in many older offices, this space is undersized and inefficient.

Another good reason to renovate is to accommodate new or upgraded equipment. Sometimes the new equipment is actually smaller, but it is deeper. Many new twelve o'clock cabinets today, for instance, take up less wall space, but when the delivery unit is factored in, they're six to twelve inches deeper. You can't just remove the old unit and pop in the new one. Sometimes the new cabinet fits in the old space but doesn't leave enough room for the doctor and the assistant to work comfortably. Or the chair may need to be moved toward the end of the room, to the point where the patient's feet hit the wall—not a good situation.

Sometimes it isn't feasible to modify the size of the room. In that case, it is important to choose equipment that works within the available space. That's when you need some expert help to take a comprehensive look at how to make the chair, the side cabinets, and the twelve o'clock unit all work.

Other renovations to accommodate equipment would include making space to accommodate a panoramic X-ray machine or a cone-beam CT scanner. Not only do these machines need more space, but they also need special electrical wiring that can get complicated. The electrical work must be up to code.

That brings us to another big reason for renovating. A dental office must be up to all sorts of codes. There's the electrical wiring, of course, which may need to be significantly upgraded when new equipment is installed. But there are other codes as well, both at the local and national level.

The accessibility standards for buildings have evolved over the years. Although the Americans with Disabilities Act did not become law until 1990, many states had accessibility requirements in place soon after Section 504 of the 1973 Rehabilitation Act became law in 1973. For many buildings constructed prior to 1973, accessibility was not a requirement.[2] Building entries and bathrooms didn't have to accommodate wheelchairs, for instance.

When older offices that were exempt from accessibility standards get renovated today, however, the ADA standards kick in. A handicap-accessible bathroom is a lot larger than a standard bathroom and eats up a lot of space. Adding access ramps, widening doorways, and other accommodations can add a lot of cost or just can't be done in the available space. ADA design standards add some expense to a project, but in the end they're not only the right thing to do but

---

2   Arlene Mayerson, "The History of the Americans with Disabilities Act," 1992, http://dredf.org/news/publications/the-history-of-the-ada/

they're also good for business. An older patient who uses a walker or wheelchair or a patient who's temporarily on crutches due to a leg injury may decide to go to the dentist down the road who makes it easier to get in the door.

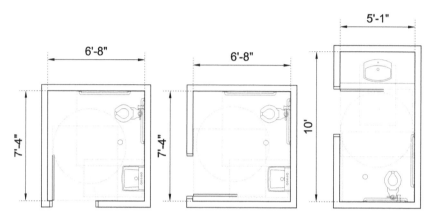

Three sample restroom configurations that meet current ADA restroom standards.

When looking at a renovation, you should start by determining if the current space is handicapped accessible. If it is not, then your architect must review your building and see what would be needed to bring your space up to code. That's complex enough, but sometimes the ADA standards allow for less than full accommodation, especially in cases of historic properties or where the cost to bring a building into full compliance exceeds 20 percent of the cost of the total project.[3] The overall idea is that you must make your best effort even if you cannot comply in full. For example, if a bathroom is too small to be wheelchair accessible, and it can't be expanded, you may be able to install grab bars to show that you've done as much as you can. These

---

3   "2010 ADA Standards for Accessible Design," Department of Justice, September 15, 2010, www.ada.gov/regs2010/2010ADAStandards/2010ADAStandards.pdf.

situations must be dealt with on a case-by-case basis. That's where it is important to work with a company with a full understanding of the ADA requirements that can help you meet those requirements (as well as all other local codes).

We had one client who wanted to move the break room and the doctor's office to the basement of the building to make room for more treatment rooms. Unfortunately, we had to tell her that it couldn't be done in that building, because the working space in the basement had to be handicapped accessible. That meant putting in an elevator, which we just couldn't get to work in the space, to say nothing of the expense. Sometimes in those situations you have the option of equal accommodation. You could provide a small break room on the main level, and then put the larger break room in the basement. But that rule is subject to the governing municipality, which might not always allow it.

Renovate or Move?

Sometimes the feasibility of a renovation dies alongside the ADA requirements. Lots of other issues can kill off the renovation idea as well, due to cost. Whenever we discuss renovation, the idea of moving to a new space instead must be considered.

The top five reasons (in no particular order) for moving to a new location instead of renovating are:

1. **The space still won't be enough.** Even with renovation, the current space won't give you what you want. If you have four operatories and want to expand to have seven, that isn't always possible. You might end up being able to add only one or two.

If you truly need or want seven, it is probably in your best interest to move to a larger space.

2. **The cost-to-benefit analysis just doesn't work.** Sometimes you can't do everything you want or need in a cost-effective way within the available space. You could even spend a lot more money and still not end up with a renovation that makes you happy. If it just can't be done well—it's time to move. We worked with one doctor who was offered the chance to buy his building for $200,000. The renovations the building needed would have cost an additional $500,000, bringing the total cost to $700,000. The alternative was to buy a building lot nearby for $100,000 and build a new building for $700,000. At the end of the day, he could spend $800,000 and have a brand-new, custom-designed office or spend $700,000 and still be in an ugly building from 1952, with low ceilings and not enough parking. In this doctor's case, this wasn't a hard decision. He chose to build his dream office.

3. **The office needs to be brought up to code.** Bringing electrical wiring, fire protection, and other infrastructure up to code can be very costly and end up eating into the office space. Moving to a space that is up to code or doesn't need much work to get it there might be a better idea, especially if the costs to update are very high.

4. **The office needs a better location.** What started out as a good location years ago might not be good anymore. Neighborhoods change, and patients may not want to come to your part of town now. Traffic patterns may have changed, making your office harder to reach. Once-attractive buildings can become dated. Especially in small towns where the growth is on the edge of town or in the suburbs, being in an old office

building downtown doesn't work anymore—now you're too far from your patient base.

5. **A major renovation would mean serious disruption to your practice.** A dentist can't just close for six weeks. A week or two is usually not a problem, but for every week you are not open, that's a week of lost income you can't get back. It's also a loss of potential new patients and even old patients. If someone needs a rush appointment or has an emergency and you're not available, that patient will go elsewhere and may not come back.

When renovating clearly isn't the solution to accommodating the growth of your practice, maybe expanding your space would work instead.

Expansion Options

Sometimes a dental practice just outgrows its current space. The most common cause is an increase in your patient base, so you need additional rooms for more hygienists. You might want to bring an associate or partner to handle more patients or make space for a specialist to come on a regular basis. Sometimes a specialist can use space on days you are not there, but there's more flexibility if you can provide dedicated rooms.

In general, there are two options for expansion: do an addition to the current building or expand into an adjoining space.

Doing an addition to your current building assumes that you own your building and the ground. If you're a tenant, it assumes your landlord is able and willing to accommodate your request to add on to the building. In either case, the first prerequisite is that there has to be room on the property to do the addition and still be compliant with all of the zoning setbacks, parking requirements, and other local regulations. When you expand your building, you want the end result to look good. The addition should look as if it was designed to be that way, not like it was an afterthought. That can sometimes be difficult. We had one client who discovered that if he expanded his office with an addition, he would get to the square footage that required installing an overhead sprinkler system for the whole building. That's a very expensive retrofit.

Before and after photos of an old gas station that was completely renovated and turned into a dental office. Two additions were added to the building, including a small entry addition on the front and a 750 square foot addition in what would become the clinical area. These additions allowed for three more treatments rooms than what the existing footprint would accommodate.

Adding clinical space means you'll probably also need to add some additional parking. The site must be evaluated to determine if it's large enough to expand and still meet your needs and the local requirements.

If there isn't enough room on the lot, the next option would be to see if any of the surrounding property can be acquired. You might be able to purchase an adjacent property and expand onto it. The drawback here is that often you're not dealing with motivated sellers. When you approach them to ask if you can buy their property to expand your own, they may see it as an opportunity to hold out for a favorable price. Or they might simply not be interested in selling.

If you lease your office space, you might be able to expand into con-tiguous space, or again, the landlord may be willing to put on an addition for you. In my experience, the stars really need to align for these options to work. You have to be in a building where there's either already vacant lease space or lease space coming available just when you need it. Even if contiguous space is available, it still might not be appropriate for expanding your practice. If the configuration isn't good, you could end up with three treatment rooms way off in the corner, a hundred feet from the sterilization center. That's not an efficient layout.

If the building is in a good location for you, and you don't want to move, you might be better off just moving into a larger space on a different floor (if it's a multi-story building). That's really the same as moving someplace else entirely, so that option must be seriously considered before making a decision. If you're in a building you like and the landlord is cooperative, this might work well.

The best reason for expanding is that you don't have to walk away from the money you've already spent on improvements. That's also the reason some owner-dentists resist the idea of moving, even when it's really the best solution. They tell me, "I spent $200,000 to build this space out nine years ago, and if I leave, I'm losing $200,000." I would argue that in some ways they are not. They have more than paid for $200,000 worth of improvements when they look at the amount of dentistry they have done over the nine years they have been there. Emotionally, though, that can be a hard pill to swallow. It's one of the big reasons we look at trying to make an expansion work, especially if the doctor likes the location.

Sometimes a landlord will say, "You can expand into the space next door, but you need to take it all." That might be more space than you want or need, but it might be the only way to expand without a move. We recently did an expansion like this. The dentist was leasing 1,800 square feet and wanted to expand. She really only needed another 1,800 square feet or so, but the bay next door was 2,500 square feet. The landlord said, "I'm not going to subdivide it any further. You know, a seven-hundred-square-foot space doesn't make any sense for me. I'd have a hard time finding a good tenant for that small space."

She decided to take the entire space. We were able to come up with a plan that made sense for her. It gave her a couple of treatment rooms she doesn't need right now, but that also means she has room for future growth. She could also look for a specialist to come and use the rooms on a regular basis. The downside is that right now she's paying rent on more space than she currently needs.

Another expansion option is to consider opening a satellite office. Instead of adding more space to their current office, some dentists will open a second (or third or more) office someplace else and see patients there as well. The dentists who do this usually have their main office in a larger metro area and open their satellite office in another prominent area in the same metro area, a nearby suburb, or in a more rural area outside the metro area. Other times doctors in rural markets sometimes choose to have satellite offices in a number of small towns. Patients who live in those areas find it easier to come to the satellite than drive forty-five minutes to get to the main office.

The drawback to a satellite office is that the dentist must commute to it a couple of times a week or hire an associate to work at the location. Some dentists are really motivated for success and don't mind the extra driving. Other dentists want to keep their life simple. They don't want to have two spaces to worry about and don't want to worry about having staff in multiple locations.

Generally speaking, satellite offices are more common for specialists. Many orthodontists, oral surgeons, endodontists, periodontists, and pediatric dentists have multiple locations.

The considerations for satellite offices include higher operating costs, as well as the construction and equipment costs associated with multiple locations versus just one. The upside is you can serve a bigger geographic area and see more patients. We work with dentists who are considering expansion to figure out the pros and cons of the satellite office alternative. It mostly comes down to the dentist's personal preferences.

Expand or Move?

When a practice needs more space, expansion is a viable option—but so is moving. How can you know which choice is better? Here are the top five reasons for moving:

1. **Your building site or lease space just doesn't work for expansion.** Sometimes expansion isn't possible—the space is too small, there's no adjacent lease space, and there's no ability to add on to the existing building. Even if you could expand, you may well outgrow the available additional space as your practice gets bigger.

2. **The cost of the expansion doesn't outweigh the upside or the return.** Additions to buildings are very costly on a square-foot basis. The scope is a lot smaller that putting up a new building, but you have to do a lot of the same work. Often, the cost of the addition won't be dollar for dollar what you would spend to build something new. It can be 25 to 50 percent more.

3. **Even with expansion, you can only have a suboptimal office layout.** The limitations of the building site or available lease space could mean you end up with a suboptimal office layout. You might get the space you need in terms of square footage and more treatment rooms, but it might have to be laid out in a way that's not good for efficient practice operations.

4. **The neighborhood has changed.** You don't want to expand further, because the neighborhood has changed or the location isn't convenient for you or your patients anymore. Moving is a good option.

5. **Expansion will disrupt your practice.** As with a major renovation, an expansion is very disruptive to your practice. The office might need to be closed for several weeks.

When expansion just isn't possible, moving or building must be considered. In many cases, a doctor may need to move to a different location but can't build a new office. They're in urban areas where no land is really available, so they have to move into leased space somewhere else. They may just prefer being in an office building with other tenants and a landlord who takes care of maintenance.

Moving a dental practice to a new space is a big undertaking. Selecting the new location and negotiating the lease is a complex task with a lot of potential pitfalls. Creating a dental office in a new leased space means basically starting from scratch. Many of the same decisions that go into deciding to build also go into deciding where to move and what the new office will look like. After considering all the factors related to moving an office and the time and costs involved, many dentists decide that building their own building is the better way to spend their money.

Lease or Build?

When renovation or expansion aren't great choices, it's time to consider building your own office. This is a big step. As an owner-dentist, this is the time to think about your vision for your future.

One of the key things to ask yourself is, "Do I see value in owning my own building? Why or why not?" I've had some doctors say, "No, I don't want to deal with it. I prefer to lease." That's understandable. Just as some dentists prefer to lease and have a landlord handle building maintenance, some dentists want to build precisely so they can control those details.

For doctors who prefer leasing but want a customized office, one leasing approach that can sometimes work really well is a "build-to-suit" lease. In this arrangement, a developer who owns (or who can purchase) the building site will build you an office to your exact specifications. Instead of owning the office, you lease it from the developer, sometimes with an option to purchase five or ten years down the road. The advantage of build-to-suit is that the landlord covers the majority of the real estate improvement costs. This allows you to use more funds for equipment, technology, and other operational expenses—very helpful for a start-up dentist. Another potential benefit to this route is it can prevent you outgrowing a smaller lease space and needing to relocate.

Before making your final decision about leasing versus building, consider all the pros and cons of both. This is a major decision that needs to be thought through very carefully, with input from your trusted advisors, including your accountant.

Leasing Pros and Cons

Leasing can have some significant advantages over building for an owner-dentist:

- *Cash availability.* Leasing requires little or no upfront cash or collateral.
- *Financial flexibility.* The cash not invested in real estate can be invested in equipment, technology, or salaries.

- *Tax advantages.* Lease payments are fully tax-deductible for the practice.
- *Low risk of obsolescence.* If the property is worth less than expected when the lease is up, then the landlord, not the dentist, bears the loss.
- *Spatial flexibility.* As your business grows, you can expand or move.
- *Mobility.* If you need to move, you don't have to deal with selling real estate.
- *Focus.* Leasing lets you concentrate on being a dentist without having to manage real estate and worry about things like snow removal, lawn care, and building maintenance.
- *Location.* Sometimes leasing can let you locate your practice in a premier location that otherwise wouldn't be affordable.

On the other hand, leasing can have some significant drawbacks:

- *No appreciation.* If the value of the property appreciates, you don't get the benefit.
- *Contractual penalties.* You can't cancel your lease agreement without penalty.
- *Less control.* In a multi-tenant building, you can't control who the other tenants are.
- *Cost.* Leasing can be more expensive than making loan payments on a building you purchase. A lease payment is forever—and most long-term leases have escalator clauses that raise the rent over time.
- *Lease renewals.* When the lease comes to an end, you need to renegotiate it all over again. If you don't have ample time

extensions negotiated into your agreement, in theory you could get forced out.

- *No equity.* When your lease expires, you have no equity in the property.

Compared to leasing, owning your own building also has its advantages and disadvantages. The advantages of owning include:

- *Ongoing costs.* Once you've paid off your building loans, you don't have any ongoing monthly building costs other than just basic maintenance and operating costs.
- *Tax savings.* Real estate owners can deduct cost recovery and mortgage interest during the holding period (when they own the property). Owning has tax benefits, such as depreciation and the way the rental income could be treated versus ordinary income—it can be more favorable.
- *Appreciation.* If property appreciates while you own it, you realize the benefit when it's sold. Owning can also be a way to diversify your investments. You're also building equity in the property while you own it.
- *Control.* As an owner-dentist, you have, to a large degree, the freedom to operate the building however you want.
- *Income.* If you have available lease space in the building, you may be able to capture some rental income.
- *Future income.* The building can become an additional income stream if you move elsewhere or retire. The space can later be rented to a younger dentist, maybe with an option to buy the building at some later date.

- *Pride of ownership.* Owning your own building feels great! And you can make the space be exactly what you want, inside and out.

But owning your building can have some significant downsides compared to leasing:

- *Cash investment.* Sometimes owning a building requires a cash down payment (10 to 30 percent of the project cost) or additional collateral. Younger dentists may find this difficult to manage.
- *Financing.* To own your building, you will probably have to borrow money for the project. The building mortgage will impact your personal balance sheet.
- *Risk.* Owning your building brings risks such as property damage, building obsolescence, or inability to sell the property at the desired price and desired time in the future.
- *Legal compliance.* As the building owner, you're responsible for compliance with laws and any associated costs, including zoning and ADA requirements.
- *Inflexibility.* If you outgrow the space or if it becomes too large, you may not be able to change the situation—you might not be able to expand the building or use less of the space.

After fully reviewing all the advantages and disadvantages of leasing and owning, you may find that you're leaning pretty strongly in one direction. No one option is best for everyone, but in my experience, especially in areas where real estate is reasonably priced, owner-dentists often decide to eventually own their office building.

Finding the Right Spot

Once the decision to build has been made, you can either look for a building to renovate, or you can build from the ground up. The first step is to identify the criteria for what you want in an office. We suggest you start the process by meeting with an experienced architect to explore your vision. What kind of architecture do you like? How many treatment rooms do you need? How much support space do you need? What is the ideal location for the new office? (We'll go into all these aspects in detail in later chapters.)

All this gives you an idea of what size the new office needs to be. If you're looking for a building to renovate or a lot for building from the ground up, you want it to be in the right area, and you want it to be the appropriate size. There's not much point in looking at buildings with twenty thousand square feet if all you need is five thousand square feet.

Location is extremely important. You want something that's in a good area with good traffic patterns. It doesn't have to be in the fanciest part of town, but it should be in a decent area, not someplace where the neighboring buildings will be run down and there are a lot of vacancies. The site also needs good visibility and good road access. You want someplace with a parking area that's easy to get in and out.

If you're looking at building to renovate, it must be one that can accommodate what you want to do. Sometimes an available building is in a good location but it's just horribly ugly. Or it might seem right, but when you take a closer look, structural issues mean it just can't be repurposed into an attractive dental office.

We find that about 40 to 50 percent of the time, a dentist just can't find an appropriate building within the desired location to buy and renovate. In that case, building from the ground up makes sense.

Should you decide to own your building, a major factor in the decision to buy or build is your ability to obtain financing. This is a very complex issue that I'll discuss in detail in chapter 3. For now, I'll just say that it's easier to get financing for a well-established, successful practice. One of the most valuable services reputable firms like Primus Dental Design & Construction often provide is helping dentists know how much to ask for based on the size and type of their practice. Often, specialty lenders who understand the business of dentistry can prepare a financing option best suited for your practice. Sometimes working with a local lender is the best option for doctors. In each specific case, it's important to make sure your lender understands your practice, your goals, and the scope of your project. With this information, they can best prepare a financing package tailored to your circumstances.

Building a dental office from the ground up is a huge commitment. From start to finish, the project can take up to two years and involve a fair amount of your time. Meetings with the real estate professionals and the architect and everyone else take time because a lot of important decisions need to be made. Your design and construction firm should be able to keep meetings and time away from the practice to a minimum, but there's still a lot of work that goes into a building project.

If you're thinking of buying and renovating a building or building something new, you have to be willing to put in the effort. Just thinking about what's involved is enough to make some people decide against it, thinking it's more than they can handle. Some dentists who didn't think building is right for them may decide to go for it after discovering all the pros and cons of the alternatives.

If a renovated or new building is what your practice really needs to thrive and grow, don't let your concerns about time, effort, and money hold you back. Work with a team that understands your goals and objectives, one that can do the research and help you with the decisions you'll need to make. You'll need to look at all your options and variables that affect them. Work with a team to look at the cost and feasibility of renovating, the cost and feasibility of expanding, and the cost and feasibility of moving. You want to make your decision based on solid information, not guesswork.

Talking It Through

We recently worked with a dentist whose practice was bursting at the seams. He was thinking of bringing in an associate, but not right away. In the meantime, he asked us to help him decide between buying the building he was in and putting an addition on it or building something new from the ground up.

The practice is in a rural area in an older building that dates back to the 1950s. The parking lot has only about half the spaces it should have. The building has low ceilings and simply isn't attractive. In addition, the site is challenging to do any work on because there's a steep hill right behind the property. The only place to put the addition he was thinking of was into the hillside. He'd have to do a lot of very expensive site preparation. The doctor wanted to know what would be involved with an expansion and if relocation would be a better idea.

We spent two months looking at both scenarios in great detail. We developed architectural plans and pricing for a renovation and expansion of his current office. Buying the building would cost about $200,000. Doing the renovations and expansion would come to about another half-million dollars. At the end of the day, after spending $700,000, the building would still date back to 1955 and in this case would still have low ceilings, inadequate parking, a dated look, and be in a part of town that was less than desirable.

We found an alternative for him: an existing vacant lot located on the major highway in town. The cost for the lot was $100,000. The cost to build the new building in the way he wanted was $725,000. In both cases, the dentist was also going to add about $300,000 in new equipment—that cost would be the same whether it was a renovation or the new building.

We looked at total cost for both options, but our financial analysis went beyond that. More importantly, we looked at what both options would mean for the dentist on a monthly basis to pay off the loans. It turned out that the loan service for the new building in the area he liked would run $900 or $1,000 more a month. We also did a cash flow analysis to show him what the projected increase in revenue would mean to his practice and his personal bottom line. For both projects, the increase in cash flow would be about the same.

The decision came down to his desire to bring in an associate in three or four years and his desire to have a more modern facility that would allow for optimal production. He decided that a new building would be more likely to attract a young doctor to his rural setting.

Chapter 2:

Location Analysis and Site Selection

Relocating your dental practice can be a complex decision. The wrong choices can have serious consequences; the right choices can lead to better patient satisfaction, a better working environment, and revenue growth.

For many dentists, the location question starts with a personal choice about where they want to be. From there, it's a matter of drilling down into the demographics of that area to find where exactly it makes the most sense to locate. Making a decision without that level of detail could mean the difference between a successful practice or one that takes a long time to reach your goals.

Demographic Analysis

Understanding the demographics of your geographic area is key to choosing your new location. Most demographic analysis is based on census data, but reputable firms also use commercial real estate information to access demographic information on any particular address or property.

For dental-specific demographic analysis, it's important to look at a lot of different factors. For example, let's say a start-up pediatric dental office needs a location. You would want to look at a number of factors, including where other pediatric dentists are located and where pediatricians and orthodontists are located, as well as where the schools are in a given market or submarket.

Overall, the demographics to focus on must reflect growth and income. You will want to know what the population growth has been recently and what the projected growth is. You will want to look at income, discretionary spending, and education. You also need to look at which dental insurers are popular in the area so the doctor can plan for what insurances to take and get credentialed for when they open the doors (if it's a start-up practice).

Demographic studies provide a snapshot of the particular area or areas where the doctor is considering locating. On a more specific and technical level, your team can use these demographic studies once they have identified potential buildings or properties or lease spaces. They would lay those addresses into the report and see how each property and location measures up relative to all the demographic data. Is the property in good proximity to neighborhoods where the median income is over $100,000? Is it far enough away from the nearest competitors that you think it'll be a good spot? What are the traffic counts at this building's intersection compared to the other two or three spots you are looking at?

The objective of the demographic studies isn't to make the final decision. Demographics are a good starting point, but they're not the end point. Based just on demographics, the analysis doesn't typically say, "Yeah, this is for sure where you should go." It just provides additional data to be analyzed. Owner-dentists should always make informed decisions, but the demographic data is only one set of information. Other factors must be assessed, like the purchase price of the property. If it's a leased space, what are the terms of the lease deal? What's the landlord willing to give you for a tenant improvement allowance at location A, versus what the landlord will offer at location B versus location C?

For instance, location A might be pretty good demographically. Location B may look even better from a demographic perspective, but the economics of location A might make it the winner. Or maybe location B may win out because it's closer to the dentist's home (if that was established as a priority).

One of the data points to look at very closely is the dentist-to-population ratio. For a general dental practice, ideally you will want there to be one dentist per 1,200 to 1,600 people or more, depending on the area. If the demographic report says in this particular location there is one dentist per seven hundred people, that's a very, very high concentration of dentists. That doesn't necessarily mean the office shouldn't go there. What it does mean is that if you're going to go there, you need to pay particular care to a number of factors, including location and signage, and you will likely need to be committed to marketing because the competition is significant compared to an area where maybe it's one dentist per 2,500 or 3,000 people. In an area where there's not a lot of competition, you're likely going to be more successful just by virtue of being there. You may not have to spend as much thought or consideration on being in a prime location when you open up an office in an underserved area.

Another filter we often lay over the demographic analysis is the number of large employers in the area. Being close to people's workplaces often means more patients because they'll come to your office before or after work if you're conveniently located. In these situations, we would also find out what dental insurance these employers offer so you can get signed up with those insurers, should you choose to do so.

The Deciding Factors

A husband-and-wife team of pediatric dentists wanted to move from Texas and open a practice in Iowa. They loved the Des Moines area, which is the largest metro area in Iowa, but beyond that basic geographic requirement they were very open about the location. They knew that there already was a strong pediatric dental presence in the region.

We were engaged to help with a demographic study and site evaluation. The first thing we did was to look at the city itself and ten of the surrounding suburbs in the metro area. We discussed which ones they would be open to being in and which were off the table. That narrowed the suburbs down to five. Then we ran a property search for all available buildings with the required square footage and look at all available lease spaces and buildings that could be purchased; in their case, they weren't interested in doing a ground-up building.

Our search initially turned up with forty-five possible spaces. The dentists shortlisted twelve properties that interested them.

We then did a drive-by of each site and further narrowed the list down to six properties.

Next, we did a demographic analysis for those six properties and found they were all located within just three communities. We looked at education levels, home ownership information, income, population growth, and so on. We were particularly interested in age, population growth, and household income because we wanted a growing area with a lot of young families with good median household incomes. Often, folks that are more affluent tend to value dental care more, so they're more likely to send their kids to a pediatric dentist instead of a general dentist. Of course, we were also mindful of where the competition was.

The demographic analysis focused our energies on three locations. Of the three, two would be good, strong places for a start-up pediatric dentist to go and have a high probability of success. One was a lease situation; the other was a purchase. We moved into financial negotiations on both.

When all the financial information for both properties was on the table, the dentists were able to easily pick the location that made the most financial sense for them: the building that was for sale. If we hadn't used the demographics to narrow down the available spaces, we would have spent a lot more time negotiating on a lot more properties. The dentists might have ended up paying a higher price to be in an area where they weren't as likely to succeed.

Careful demographic analysis helped this pediatric dental office choose an ideal location in an affluent, high-growth suburb with a large number of children.

We did most of this project from a distance, while the clients were still busy with their practice in Texas. They only came to Iowa once during the site selection process, to tour the final three properties. From the time they said they wanted to move to Des Moines to opening the doors was about a twelve-month process. They're in a beautiful space they love, and they've done very well from the day they opened.

The demographic analysis really helped them get close to a good final decision quickly. In a small area, owner-dentists often don't need to do an extensive demographic study to pin things down, but in a larger metro areas like Des Moines, Denver, Kansas City, or Minneapolis, a more in-depth analysis is really helpful for the decision-making process.

Selecting the Site

A demographic analysis is the right starting point for picking the general area for a practice. Once that area has been selected, we use a more detailed site selection analysis to find the best location within that area.

A challenge for some dentists is finding sites that are small enough for them. In a lot of areas, the available properties are bigger than they need. Most new dental offices need between half an acre and an acre and a half of land for the construction of their building and parking area. Lots of available commercial parcels are too large. That means part of what your team must look for are sites that are small enough or sites that can be subdivided for your purposes.

The other alternative is for you to play the role of a developer. In that case, you're more willing to buy a larger piece of property and deal with the excess land, either by reselling it immediately or holding on to it for down the road. In most situations, owner-dentists may find it is in their best interest to focus on their core business first. Being a developer can come later, once your new practice is well established.

When looking at properties, the first thing to consider is whether the properties are priced appropriately given your financial situation. A site may be in your ideal demographic area, and it may be the right size, but if it's $30 per square foot instead of $10 or $15, you may have to cross it off the list, or you may need to consider a lease situation for that location instead of a purchase.

In terms of site criteria, look for sites that have good access. The parking lot must be easy to get in and get out of for patients. You also want good visibility from the road so patients can see your building or your signage. Oftentimes, the most visible and most accessible sites (especially in premier locations) cost substantially more than other sites. In nearly every case, there's a balancing act as you evaluate a given location, and you must carefully consider how much a site is really worth to you and your practice. Your team can help as you weigh various options. Ideally, great visibility can be achieved at a cost that works within the total budget; however, that's not usually the case in bigger markets.

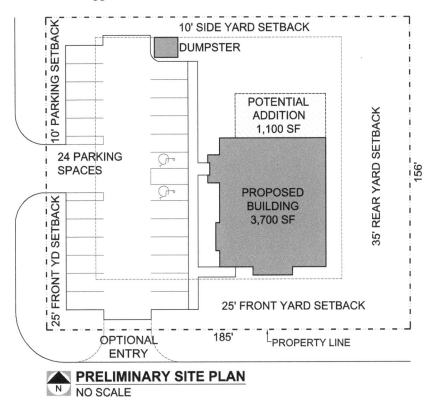

PRELIMINARY SITE PLAN
NO SCALE

A site plan showing a proposed dental office, building addition, parking area, sidewalks, dumpster, and entry drives. Note the site setbacks shown on the site plan that dictate where parking areas and the building can be located.

Consider looking for sites where the utilities are already run to the property or are close enough for easy hook-up. Ideally, the water line, sewer line, and other utilities are installed to the property lines or are in close proximity to them. The cost to extend utilities to a property can add up in a hurry. We've looked at sites that seemed too good to be true on paper and were priced very attractively, only to find that the cost to install the water and sewer lines was going to add another $90,000 to the purchase price. Always verify the availability of utilities and infrastructure to a site before making a buying decision.

Infrastructure First

A few years ago, a doctor bought a property before he hired us to design the building and do the site design. During the course of our work, we discovered that the property didn't have water or sewer lines. The nearest water and sewer lines were about three hundred feet away, in the middle of the street. We would have to cut into the street to extend the lines. The cost to do that was going to be about $60,000. Obviously, if he had known that before buying the lot, he could have negotiated a better price. The additional costs could have been problematic for him, but we were able to help by working with the city to get them to cover about $50,000 of the cost. It took a fair amount of time and effort, but we were able to keep the cost of this situation to a minimum.

A site analysis must include your personal preferences. Many dentists want to be on the ground floor of an office building; others don't want to be in a building with another dentist. One of our clients really wanted a building that looked modern and contemporary with an entrance directly from the parking lot, instead of an interior vestibule with a hallway leading to the office doors. Those two factors eliminated 80 percent of the properties on the market that could work for him. Other desired features including wanting some green space or a water feature next to the office. As you can well imagine, there aren't tons of properties with those types of features. We do our best to search out and evaluate properties that meet whatever criteria are really important to the dentist.

Site Selection and Utility Costs

A doctor in South Dakota was relocating his office within the same town. After looking at the handful of available existing buildings, he decided that to achieve the modern look and feel he was hoping for, it was in his best interest to find vacant ground and build a new building.

We identified two pieces of property that could work for him. Option 1 would cost $150,000; option 2 would cost $75,000. The locations were comparable in terms of visibility and access, so naturally the dentist was drawn to option 2 because of the lower price.

We did site layouts to show how both sites could work. There were no issues—both sites could work and easily accommodate his building and parking area. Then we moved on to analyzing the sites for the availability of utilities and site access. That's when we discovered that option 2 didn't have water or sewer lines installed to the property. The cost to run water was going to be $50,000, and the cost to run sanitary sewer was going to be $25,000. Additionally, the city told us that the current access road to the site wasn't built to city standards and couldn't be used. It needed to be ripped out and reinstalled! The cost to bring the road up to city standards was going to be another $35,000. At the end of the day, the less expensive lot ended up costing an additional $110,000 to get it to the same development position that the more expensive lot was in already. The site analysis concluded that the more expensive lot would actually end up saving him about $35,000 to $40,000.

Chapter 3:

Negotiating the Move

After you have located the property for your office, the next step is to negotiate the lease or the purchase price for the building or land. This can get very complex—as the example of the dentist who bought land not realizing it needed utility lines shows, expert advice can make the process go a lot more smoothly, with no unpleasant surprises.

Negotiating a Lease

Based on demographics and the site analysis, the best option for you may be leased space. Once you and your team have identified the possible spaces that could work for you, the next step is to negotiate the best possible deal with the landlord.

In many ways, dentists are in a very strong negotiating position for leased space. Dentists are very appealing tenants because they have a low failure rate—nationally, fewer than 1 percent fail. The landlord can count on income stability, a very attractive idea. Dentists also aren't disruptive to other tenants in the building, they have normal hours of operation, they attract a safe clientele, and they give the building a nice professional image. Also, once they move to a new office, dentists tend to stay put for a while; the landlord can count on you as a good long-term tenant.

On the other hand, a dental office has some drawbacks for a landlord. It needs more parking spaces than some general office users, sometimes more than the square footage of the office entitles them to. That can cause conflicts with the other tenants. Dental offices need a lot of costly improvements, so the landlord many times has to provide a higher tenant improvement allowance for these things. And all those changes mean that if the dentist does vacate the space, the landlord will have to go to a lot of expense to modify the office for the next tenant (if that tenant isn't another dentist).

Overall, the plus side of having a good, reliable, long-term tenant usually makes landlords very willing to negotiate. Your team should begin the space search by examining listing data for potential properties. Look at items such as the published lease rate, the published tenant improvement allowance if there is one, the common area maintenance costs, and the taxes.

The next step is to have your representative submit a Request for Proposal (RFP) to the landlords. The RFP asks for a description of what the landlord is willing to do for you in terms of rent, improvements, and so on. It's important to maintain a level of confidentiality at this point by not revealing much about the intended user. If you're currently in a lease space and you're making an offer on another lease space, there's a chance that the building owners might know each other, especially in a small town. You just don't want that information to get out or be gossiped about, so confidentiality is important.

The objective with the RFP is to get the landlord to lay out the proposed economics of that particular space. If the landlord states what he's willing to do first, then you can offer a counter-proposal. In many cases, it becomes a back-and-forth process of negotiation until both parties can agree on the terms of the deal. Generally speaking, the longer the lease term, the more favorable economics can be for the dentist.

A major point of negotiation is the tenant improvement allowance. The costs of improvements for dental space compared to a general office are significantly higher. In fact, they're about double in most markets across the country. Often, landlords and real estate brokers don't know that or don't necessarily understand that, so you and your team may have to educate them about costs.

For start-up practices, negotiating an adequate improvement allowance is crucial. Given the loan limits for most dental start-ups, you may not have enough money to do the build-out and also buy the new equipment and technology, do advertising and marketing, and provide some working capital for the practice. For most start-ups, a really important part of the negotiation is getting the tenant improvement allowance as high as possible so the project can happen.

For established practices, the improvement allowance often isn't as critical an item. It sometimes makes sense to ask the landlord to quote a rental rate with a tenant improvement allowance and a rental rate without a tenant improvement allowance. This gives you the ability to evaluate what's more important and more feasible in your specific situation. In many cases, an established doctor can borrow money for the improvements at a lower rate than what the landlord will charge.

Those improvements can then be amortized over the life of the lease. Your team can help you look at both options. You can then decide if you'd rather have the landlord provide the financing for that portion of the project or if you'd rather just have your bank do it—or if it might not even be better to just pay for it out of pocket.

The lease negotiations take into account how competitive the local market is. If there's a lot of vacant space and very little activity, landlords will tend to be more aggressive with their tenant improvement allowances. If it's a hot market with lots of activity, they're less likely to be aggressive or provide more. Another variable is the specific financial situation of the building owner. Some building owners and developers have deeper pockets and are able to provide more to get a desirable long-term tenant.

Because they're spending so much to improve the space, landlords often want dentists to sign long-term leases, sometimes as long as ten to fifteen years. In many cases, dentists are fine with this because they don't want the hassle and expense of moving after five years. If you do need to move to a bigger space, sometimes the landlord can be a solution. If the landlord owns multiple properties, they have the opportunity to secure a tenant for a long time in a new location.

In many markets, dentists are such desirable tenants that landlords will compete to get them. It's typically in your best interest to look at multiple options. Submit RFPs for at least two properties so you can compare the economics. Sometimes the numbers end up making the decision, especially when there's not that much difference among the locations.

Another deal point that can be negotiated is when you start paying rent. The landlord obviously wants to start collecting rental income as soon as possible, but you may want to start paying rent only when you can see patients in the new space. The negotiation of the free rent period is important. The landlord wants to see rent commence as soon as you "occupy" the space, meaning as soon as you start working on the improvements. The case can be made that you're not generating revenue yet, so rent shouldn't begin until construction is completed. You can't always get landlords to agree to this, but in some markets you can negotiate thirty to ninety days of free rent, sometimes even longer.

Who does the improvements is another negotiating point. In some instances, landlords prefer to work with their own architect and contractors. Some architects and contractors don't have the specialized knowledge needed for building a dental office, and hiring them to complete your dental office can be problematic. If the landlord insists on using his or her own people, you have a decision to make. Is this still a space you want, knowing that the build-out will be done by the landlord's contractor who has no knowledge of dental construction? In some cases, if the landlord insists, and the location and economics are far and away the best, this may be a compromise you're willing to make. However, for most landlords, the priority is securing rental income for their space. If you make them choose between getting the tenant and having somebody else do the build-out versus not getting the tenant at all, they'll generally be willing to let you use your own dental-specific architect and contractor. It's your office— insist on working with the team you choose, not someone without the expertise needed to design and build your office correctly.

Once you've reached an agreement, both parties sign a letter of intent to lease. This normally isn't legally binding on either party—it's simply a document stating the terms of the agreement as understood by both parties. The landlord then uses it to prepare the lease agreement.

Once you receive the draft lease from the landlord, your real estate professional and/or your attorney should review the lease to make certain that the terms agreed upon in the letter of intent were put into the lease document. You will also want to be sure certain provisions that are common in some leases are not in your lease agreement, specifically clauses that give the landlord the right to move you to a new location should they desire to do so. Most commercial leases that have such a clause state the landlord must pay for all the costs associated with the move, but the disruption that a forced move can cause your practice is something that should be avoided at all costs! Be certain any language to this effect is removed from your lease agreement. Also, leases often seek to limit the transfer of ownership within the entity that's leasing a space (your practice). Depending on how strongly the lease language is worded, this can effectively limit your ability to sell a portion, or all, of your practice without your landlord's approval. Be certain that your representatives modify or remove any language that would prevent you from making such changes in your practice—your landlord shouldn't have control over these types of decisions.

The Build-Out

We went through a situation recently with a doctor who wanted to work with us, but the landlord was insisting on doing the build-out. The doctor gave me permission to talk with the landlord. We talked first about some of the other items related to the project. When we got around to the improvements, he said, "Well, I really want to do the improvements." I replied, "I appreciate you saying that, but you have no dental or medical experience. Our client is really concerned about that, given the highly specialized nature of the improvements he needs. He likes your building, but there are other buildings that are workable for him so who does the build-out is going to be very important." The landlord recognized the possibility of losing the tenant and immediately said, "Well, that's fine. We don't need to do the build-out."

Negotiating Land and Building Purchases

The negotiations for purchasing a building or a building lot are pretty similar—and similarly complex. Bringing experienced advisors and real estate professionals in at the start is key; this isn't something you should do without expert advice.

The starting point for a purchase is similar to a lease negotiation. After site evaluation has been performed, you can usually narrow the options down to one to three good choices. From there, it's a matter of deciding which property or properties to make an offer on.

The negotiations begin with a letter of intent to purchase or a purchase agreement that lays out the basic points of the transaction. At this point, discretion is very important because in many cases when a seller sees that a dentist is looking to buy his building or property, any sort of ability to negotiate goes out the window. When the doctor is the one driving around and calling on the spaces, they're dealing with professionals that negotiate these types of transactions for a living. Unfortunately, they often take advantage of the doctor's inexperience.

We suggest that offers submitted for doctors be done anonymously, if it all possible. They can come from a generic real estate entity (a dummy corporation) that can't be directly linked to the doctor. Many sellers are fine negotiating a sale without knowing who the end user is, at least initially. Sometimes they want to know that it's a legitimate use and is being bought by a real person. Have your representative reveal only enough to give them the confidence to proceed with the transaction.

A critical item to include in the purchase agreement is a provision that lets you or whomever is buying on your behalf walk away should any issue come up in the due diligence period. Ideally, the language is open-ended enough so if you decide a property isn't a good fit two months down the road, you can walk away from the purchase and get your earnest money back. A lot can go wrong during the due diligence period before closing, so you want to be able to get out of the purchase agreement easily, if necessary.

In the due diligence period you may discover things about the property that weren't previously known. For example, a few years ago, we helped a doctor buy a property. It seemed like a great deal, but when we performed the Phase I environmental assessment, we discovered that from 1950 to 1980 there was a body shop on the property. Because of this type of use, we then had to do a Phase II environmental site assessment using an environmental specialist, which was much more intensive and much more expensive. Thankfully, the samples showed no contamination of the soil or groundwater, so the doctor was able to move forward. If a problem had come up, we would have been able to back out of the deal without losing her earnest money.

Another pitfall during due diligence is that the local authorities may not approve the site plan that's presented or may force you to make modifications to accommodate their requests. Sometimes they'll put additional architectural requirements on a building. They may say, "This is going to be in our new design overlay district, so we want you to put 75 percent masonry on all four sides of the building." The additional cost to conform to their requirements may be $40,000 to $50,000. Depending on your budget, that may or may not matter, but these types of requirements can come up.

If it's a property that must be rezoned, the rezoning may be denied. If you really want the site, you can fight for the zoning, but often a zoning denial is a good reason to look harder at one of the other possible properties instead. Thankfully, this is not a very common issue, because for the most part, zoning boards view dentists as desirable users and want to accommodate them.

Similarly, dentists sometimes buy bigger lots than they require, often with the intent to subdivide. This process can take months—new legal descriptions must be drawn up, surveys must be done, and the municipality must approve the subdivision. If for some reason it turns out that the property can't be subdivided, though, you want to be able to back out of the purchase. Be sure contingencies addressing these items are in your purchase agreement.

Walking Away

We had a property under contract for a doctor last year. All design work was done, everything was priced, he was set to close on the building in two weeks, and we were set to start construction the following week. Then he got a call from his dental school classmate in Indiana. This old friend offered him a 50 percent partnership in his practice. Because the doctor's wife really wanted to move back to Indiana, he took the offer. Thankfully, there was a strong "out" clause in the purchase agreement. He was able to walk away, get his $5,000 earnest money back, and move forward with the opportunity in Indiana.

Timing Is Everything

One of the hardest parts of purchasing a property is getting the timing right so that the financing falls into place easily. Sellers usually want you to buy and close on a property quickly, but the truth is you typically need no less than ninety days, and in some cases as many as 180 days, to work through all of the necessary steps. Just the approval process for planning and zoning commissions can take three to four months. The reality of creating design documents, getting necessary regulatory and financing approvals, conducting the environmental assessments, and wrapping up all the details takes time, often four to six months.

Sometimes it pays to buy the land just to tie it up. You might not be to the point of needing to build a new office, but there's land available in an ideal location. You might buy it now and hold onto it for building a few years down the road. This is fairly common, particularly in an area where there aren't a lot of good land options. When something becomes available, you may want to jump on it.

For most doctors, it's most advantageous to buy the land or the building and simultaneously close on the construction loan. The cash requirements for buying raw land are very different than buying a building and opening a construction loan. Typically, if you're buying just land, a bank is going to want 20 to 40 percent of the land purchase price in cash. If you're buying a $300,000 piece of property, that could be as much as $120,000 down. But if you're buying the land in conjunction with starting your project, you'll probably need to contribute only anywhere from 25 percent to as little as nothing. Getting the timing right could be the difference between writing no check and writing a check for $120,000.

62

Chapter 4:

Financing Your Growth

Few dentists have any practical experience with the complicated issue of financing practice growth. To do this successfully, professional help from experienced advisors is essential, including your accountant, financial advisor, and lenders familiar with you and/or your industry.

To Finance or Not to Finance

The first decision that must be made regarding the financing of your project is whether you want to finance it at all. In many cases, doctors choose to lease their office space—whether it be an existing building, portion of a building, or a custom build-to-suit office designed and built specific to the doctor's requests. The pros and cons of this option have already been discussed in chapter 3, but again, the decision to lease versus own must be made prior to beginning the project. In some cases, doctors choose to consider both options. Depending on your circumstances and long-term goals, it may be prudent to do so.

When arranging for financing for anything from a renovation to a completely new building, many factors beyond the basic interest rate must be considered. The first step, before approaching the bank, is to look at your creditworthiness. Talk to your accountant and financial advisors to get an accurate picture. A loan obviously has cash and debt implications, but there are also less-obvious tax implications that vary depending on the types of loans available. Bear in mind that the more money you want to borrow, the more the bank will want to know about your financial situation. You may need to be able to show enough cash or collateral to support the loan amount, or, if working with a bank that understands the business of dentistry, you will need to have a practice that is strong enough to support the amount of money you wish to borrow.

A strong practice also helps with the loan amount. In fact, when you work with a specialty dental lender, the strength of the practice may be even more important than your tangible assets. Talk with your trusted financial advisors and look carefully at your practice. In particular, you want to look at your year-over-year growth in collections, active patients, and new patients. If these numbers are showing a steady upward trend, you can likely move ahead with some confidence.

If there's a problem with your credit, you may be able to fix it. You may find, however, that your current financial position just isn't good enough to be asking for a substantial loan. Especially if you're relatively new to practicing dentistry, you may be better off waiting a few more years to improve your overall financial picture.

Where to Start

The starting point for financing is often your local bank. A bank can give you an idea of the amount you can reasonably expect to borrow based on your current financial position, including existing personal and practice debt. The bank will also look at your cash position and other assets such as investments, life insurance, and your house. When it comes to collateral, most local banks are only interested in cash or liquid assets.

A trusted team will provide an accurate picture of what you can realistically afford to do. Sometimes, after analyzing your practice revenues and the anticipated project costs, you may discover the project should be scaled back. To make the project work, for instance, that perfect piece of property for $600,000 may have to be replaced by the lot a few blocks away that's going for $400,000. Sometimes you may discover that now isn't the best time for a project at all—you may need to wait until you and your practice are in better financial shape.

Truth be told, once young doctors begin practicing, they have the potential to earn significant income. Although it can be difficult, resisting the urge to buy a big house and nice cars early in your career can ensure that you have the financial strength you need should you want to invest in your practice. If you're thinking of buying a practice, starting your own, buying all new dental equipment, or building a new office, it is important to have some cash to show the bank.

Young doctors often feel that their first priority should be to pay off all of their student loan debt. Actually, most banks—especially dental-specialty lenders—expect you to have some student loan debt. They don't expect you to have that paid off all your student loan debt in five years. In fact, in some cases, it would be better for you to save some money rather than pay off all your student loan debt. That saved money shows liquidity, which is an important concept to the bank. This may sound counterintuitive, and the right balance is different for everyone. Be sure your advisors know your long-term objectives so that they can counsel you in this area.

Make your monthly loan payments on schedule, but depending upon your situation, it may not be a good idea to go beyond that if you're planning to open an office or make substantial investments in your practice. A few years ago we worked with a young doctor who only had $70,000 in loans left five years after finishing school. The problem was, because he had paid down his student loan so aggressively, he didn't have much in cash or savings. The bank turned down his loan request, saying he should have accumulated more money after working for five years. This may seem strange, but it is often the case.

In most cases, the bank will say to you, "Yes, we think you're a good borrower. Let's talk more." The next step depends on whether you're a start-up practice or an established practice. For the start-up, the lender is looking for a modest level of liquidity, a good credit score, and no issues with your dental license. In most cases, a start-up will be able to get project loans ranging from $350,000 to $600,000, depending on whether you're a general dentist or a specialist.

For an existing practice, the lender looks at your practice revenues over the past two to three years. The loan amount the lender will be likely to approve is based on the historic revenue, generally in the range of about 1.5 to 2 times your annual collection amount. So if your practice collects $1 million a year, it's reasonable to assume that a bank would approve you for a $1.5 million to $2 million total project, including land, design fees, construction, dental equipment, technology, and furnishings. Some lenders are more lenient. We've seen the ratio go as high as 2.5 to 3 times collections or even a bit higher, but these are less-common scenarios and are based largely on the projected growth of the practice, current profitability of the practice, existing debt and the financial strength of the borrower.

For an existing practice, the bank will want to see your personal financial statement and have you fill out a loan application. For a start-up, the bank often wants to see a business plan with some cash flow projections. They might also want to a competition analysis and a marketing plan.

When you're preparing to seek financing, it's important to understand all the costs that will be part of your project. There's more to it than just the improvements and the equipment or the land. The biggest issue with many doctors planning their growth is that they often woefully underestimate on the front end. Work with your team to make sure your budget is accurate before going to the bank.

Professional Design Fees (architectural, engineering, structural)	$
Due Diligence Costs (soil testing, environmental testing, asbestos testing)	$
Construction	$
Land	$
Dental Equipment & Dental Cabinetry	$
Furniture & Décor	$
Telephone System	$
Office Equipment	$
Window Treatments	$
Appliances	$
Computer Hardware	$
Computer Software	$
Dental Instruments/Small Equipment	$
Dental Supplies/Merchandise	$
Audio Visual	$
Signage	$
Security System	$
Cabling System	$
Working Capital (for payroll, marketing, rent deposit, insurance, stationary, etc.)	$
Total Budget	**$**

A sample project budget broken down by the primary categories of a project.

Lender Options

Although the starting point for financing a dental office project is often your local bank, it's not the only option to consider. Working with the right lender can make the difference between a project that gets off the ground and one that doesn't. In many cases, the right lender isn't the local bank. It's often a dental-specialty lender that understands what makes sense and what doesn't for dental practices in terms of loan amount, debt load, and all the other ins and outs of lending to dentists.

Local banks are asset-based lenders and look primarily at the value of the property and your assets when deciding on the loan amount. In some cases, your local lender can be a good option because if you bank there, they already know you and have a good understanding of your financial situation. Sometimes that means they're able to accommodate specific requests for your loan that maybe a larger lender can't. The drawback to your local bank is that they don't necessarily know much about dental projects or dental buildings. Specifically, they don't know that in many instances (as often as 75 percent of the time), these projects will not appraise for what they cost. This can be a real problem for a growing practice because the loan proposals are usually structured so that the bank lends you a certain percentage—80, 85, or 90 percent—of the appraised value. But what happens when the building appraises for only 90 percent of the cost?

Let's say you're doing a $1 million project, and the bank has said they'll loan you 80 percent of the costs. That means you must be prepared to contribute $200,000. But if that $1 million project then appraises for $900,000 and they'll still only loan you 80 percent of the appraised value, that means the maximum loan amount is now $720,000. You now would have to contribute $280,000 instead of the original $200,000. The worst part of this situation is that the appraisal for a project typically comes in only a week or two before closing. You don't know for sure what your cash requirement is until the very last minute. There's a fair amount of risk to you in this scenario.

Ideally, you would get the local bank to agree to either waive that requirement or come up with a secondary loan source to cover the shortfall. It's in your best interest to negotiate for that contingency early in the process.

If your local lender won't work with you on the above issues, a better option in these situations may be working with a specialty dental lender. These banks are very familiar with the issues in dental lending, such as the appraised value problem, and are oftentimes able to work out solutions that local banks will not. Dental-specific lenders will often consider longer fixed-rate periods for the loans they offer, another factor to consider when evaluating your options.

Currently, the leading lender (based on loan volume) in the dental area is Bank of America Practice Solutions. Other prominent dental-specific lenders include Wells Fargo, PNC, US Bank, and Live Oak Bank. Each of these banks has divisions that work specifically with healthcare and dental professionals. They understand the business of dentistry and often provide quick turnarounds for loan requests.

Once you have your loan proposals in hand, your advisors should help you evaluate the pros and cons of each. Again, your team should be involved, as they see dozens of these proposals each year and can help you understand exactly what you're committing to with each option.

Small Business Administration Loans

A potential source of financing that's often overlooked is the US Small Business Administration (SBA). The SBA was set up in 1953 as an independent agency of the federal government to aid, counsel, assist, and protect the interests of small business concerns. The SBA doesn't actually make direct loans to small businesses—instead, it guarantees loans made to small business owners by banks and other lenders. So if you apply for an SBA loan, you're still actually applying for a commercial loan through a bank. Some people believe, because of the parameters of SBA loans, they can't work for dental projects.

Because of their structure, SBA loans are great for owner-occupied projects, which dental projects are. They require a lot less cash on the front end. Most will cover 85 or 90 percent of the costs, as opposed to most conventional loans, which only cover 75 to 80 percent. Along with the lower up-front cash requirement, however, come substantial fees. The loan fees could run to $20,000 to $50,000, compared to much less for a conventional loan. But the tradeoffs of lower cash requirements, and often a good long-term fixed interest rate for a portion of the loan, make exploring this option worthwhile.

SBA loans fall into two main categories, 504 loans and 7A loans. The 504 loan is a loan partnered with a local bank. The SBA carries 40 percent of the loan, and the local bank carries 50 percent. Local banks love 504 loans because they only have a 50 percent position in the project—their risk is lower. The 40 percent loan from the SBA can have anywhere from a ten- to a twenty-year fixed interest rate, which banks also love. The downside is there's a ten-year graduated pre-payment penalty for the SBA portion of the loan. Also, the interest rate on the SBA portion of the loan doesn't lock until a few months after the project is done, so you don't know your final interest rate until around a year after the project starts.[4] That opens you to some interest rate risk.

SBA 7A loans[5] have similar cash requirements on the front end. There's only a three-year graduated pre-payment penalty, and the

---

4   "CDC/504 Loan Amounts," SBA, www.sba.gov/content/cdc504-loan-amounts-repayment-terms-interest-rates-fees.

5   "General Small Business Loans: 7(a)," SBA, www.sba.gov/7a-loan-program

interest rate is established and locks on the front end of the loan, as opposed to the back end. The maximum loan amount is $5,000,000.

There are some big advantages to an SBA loan. The main one is that the SBA allows the loan with 10 percent down, with all fees and costs being financed by the lender. Sometimes an SBA lender will work with a partner bank and can count the partner bank's contribution toward the real estate project. This, in turn, covers the equity requirement by the bank and the SBA, enabling financing for 100 percent of the project cost.

While applying for an SBA loan involves a lot more paperwork (the stack of forms is often three inches thick), these loans offer greater flexibility, a longer term for repaying the loan, little or no down payment, mitigation for appraisals, and no covenants. In most instances, the trade-off makes SBA lending a good option to consider.

To qualify for an SBA loan, you must show that the money will lead to employment growth through expanding your business. Some pretty strict rules apply:

- The business must be organized and operated for profit. No nonprofit firms can borrow.
- SBA loans can't be used for refinancing existing debt.
- For a building loan, the small business must occupy 51 percent of the space for a building purchase and 60 percent for new construction.
- Companies with a net worth of more than $6 million are ineligible.

SBA loans are particularly valuable when a commercial bank loan won't cover all the costs and the doctor needs to put in a lot of cash. An SBA loan can be great way to get around this deal-breaking requirement.

Alternative Financing

Sometimes it's possible to sidestep banks completely. Alternative financing for the project could come from a family member in a position to help, for example. We've seen situations where well-situated parents will finance the building project for a dentist. Sometimes, alternative financing comes in the form of a developer willing to do a turnkey project or a build-to-suit project for you. As mentioned earlier, developers will sometimes agree to a lease-to-own arrangement, where a portion of your lease payments goes toward a future purchase. There's an option for you to purchase the building maybe seven to ten years down the road. It's not really financing—it's another way to get the building without having to write the check.

A build-to-suit office can be a good option if owning a building isn't the right decision for the owner-dentist.

Especially in rural areas that need to attract practitioners, grants or forgivable loans may be available. Sometimes, local economic development boards will provide low-interest loans to doctors. And then there are area-specific programs, like the one in northwest Iowa that gives you a substantial grant if you design your building using a Dutch architectural style, in keeping with the area's history. It's not financing per se, but $30,000 to $50,000 toward construction costs is very nice to have.

Some areas of the country offer either tax abatement or tax increment financing (TIF). Basically, they're offering you a rebate on future tax payments on the project. All these offers are to entice you to relocate in their town or area so that the residents can access dental services. Some places offer substantial tax breaks if you locate in a revitalization area. These can be very good deals because often we can get a good price on an older building that is dilapidated but fundamentally in reasonable condition. We can rehab these buildings, bring them up to code, give the doctor a great new office, and improve the neighborhood while saving money.

Is Now the Right Time?

The big question that doctors must ask themselves regarding financing is, is it right for you? Is now the right time? Are you comfortable borrowing $500,000 to $2.5 million? How comfortable are you spending a lot of money to acquire real estate or do a project? Would you feel more comfortable if you remained a tenant? If you are a start-up practice, taking on $400,000 to $500,000 in debt, maybe on top of $300,000 in student loans, when you don't have a guaranteed income, can be challenging. It's not for everybody. There may be nothing wrong with deciding to hold off for a few years. It depends on your goals and what you ultimately decide is best for you.

Chapter 5:

Design Steps from the Ground Up

The decision to build a new office has been made, the site has been located, and the financing is in place. Now, it's time to begin the design process.

Tenant build-outs and extensive renovations usually require some if not all of the same considerations as building from the ground up. Existing conditions must be verified, areas for improvement such as HVAC identified, and all necessary permitting and municipal approvals must be obtained.

The particular design needs of a dental practice (special plumbing, dedicated electrical circuits, sterilization and lab space, room for growth, and so on) must be considered at every point.

All this can seem overwhelming at first, but having a good idea of what goes into each step makes the process much easier to understand. Guidance from the team you've chosen to work with helps to ensure that every design step is done exactly as it should be. This is another key area where dental-specific experience really counts.

Choosing the Architect

A dental office is a highly specialized space. Many of the things specific to a dental office aren't found in any other type of use. In addition, there are critical space relationships that must be maintained and specific site layout considerations that must be contemplated when the floor plan and site plan are developed. The goal is a design that functions at an optimal level of comfort, patient safety, access, and efficiency.

We strongly advise dentists to hire only a highly experienced architect. Hiring someone who has little or no dental experience puts you at risk for a bad outcome. I believe the last thing a dentist wants to be doing is educating their design professional on the spaces that are required for their office to function. If the design firm doesn't know what a sterilization room is or doesn't know what a statim is used for or doesn't know the importance of the location of the X-ray machine in the office, the design will be bad. You wouldn't go to your family doctor and ask him to extract a wisdom tooth. You'd go to a well-qualified, experienced dentist. It's the same with the architect and other design professionals: training and experience really count.

You don't want to educate your design professionals. It should be the other way around: they should educate you about great ideas for improving the efficiency and comfort of your office.

When trying to decide on a design firm to work with for your dental office, a good starting point is to talk with other members of your advisory team. Oftentimes, your dental supply representative or dental CPA is familiar with firms who specialize in dental offices. Once you have a recommendation, start asking questions. Have they done dental projects? What size and type of dental projects have they completed? How many dental projects have they completed? How recently? Do they have photos you can see?

The next step is crucial: you must ask if you can talk to past clients. Don't just get the names and drive past the offices or look at photos. Check the references personally. Call these people. Find out what their experience was like working with the architect or design firm. Were they timely in the plans? Did they meet the dates and deadlines? Did they understand your vision and give you want you wanted? Did they stay within the budget? Were there a lot of change orders during the construction? What was the overall experience like?

Deciding whom you're going to work with on your project is a lot like a marriage. It's important that there is a good fit. You must be able to relate to the people, you must know that they understand you, and you must see yourself capable of interacting with them frequently for a while, because you will be. An architect could be very talented and have an amazing portfolio, but if he's not a nice person, you may not want to spend ten to twenty hours in a room with him over the next couple of months.

Does it matter where your architect is located? Must he or she be nearby? Not necessarily. You want an architect with a lot of dental office experience and who is compatible with you and easy to work with. With today's computer-assisted drafting and instant communications, working with someone out of your area is easier than ever. The one drawback is that you or the firm you hire may still need to engage a local architect to ensure that the design is compliant with the local codes. An architect in Florida can't be expected to know and comply with all of the local codes in Indiana. Architects partner with their local colleagues all the time for exactly this reason, so this isn't really a problem. One simple way to avoid this issue is to ask the architect you're considering where they are licensed and how they handle local code issues when working in other states.

Working with the Architect

The architectural design process can only go forward with a lot of input from you. The formal design process begins by you meeting with your architect to discuss the project in great detail, a process called "programming."

The American Institute of Architects defines programming as follows: *architectural programming* is the thorough and systematic evaluation of the interrelated values, goals, facts, and needs of a client's *organization, facility users, and the surrounding community. A well-conceived program* leads to high-quality design.[6]

The groundwork you laid when you first establishing your project goals (Vision Casting—discussed in chapter 1) will prove valuable as the programming begins. Discussing and establishing space requirements for your dental office is one of the primary priorities of programming. This process is also structured to help your architect understand what's important to you and your practice in terms of both design and function. The end result of programming is essen-

---

6   Robert G. Hershberger, "Programming," *The Architect's Handbook of Professional Practice, 13th edition*, 2000, www.aia.org/aiaucmp/groups/aia/documents/pdf/aiab089267.pdf.

tially a "treatment plan" for the design of your office. From here, your architect can begin developing concepts for your office for your review. In most cases, the doctor must meet with the design team in a series of three to four meetings, lasting anywhere from two to four hours each, over the course of two to three months. There's a lot to cover! In many cases, the first meeting is in person, but it doesn't have to be. Subsequent meetings can either be in person or over the phone, depending upon your preference.

An important point to remember about the design process is that everything in it ties together. A change in one aspect cascades down and can affect everything else. For instance, civil engineering can't begin until you've approved a concept design for the site. Structural design and mechanical and electrical and plumbing design can't start until the floor plan has been developed and you have signed off on it. The building elevations must be approved to finalize the design of the structure. Getting all the design documents correctly prepared by all the different design disciplines usually takes more than five hundred hours for a ground-up dental office.

Up to a point, changes to the design are normal and should be expected. Once the preliminary design is finalized, however, changes to the design can be more involved and impact multiple design disciplines involved in the project. Keep in mind that dramatic design changes late in the process can delay your project—avoid big changes late in the process, if at all possible.

Siting the Building

If you're building a new office, the location of your building on the site you've selected is an important element to consider. As you evaluate site options, in many cases your architect will prepare a preliminary site layout that takes into account all of the factors for a particular property. The idea is to show how a building and parking space would fit onto the site and whether or not the particular site would work well. This process can quickly eliminate some sites and give you a good idea of which of the remaining sites is best.

Where the new building is located on the site depends a lot on what a given municipality requires. A number of things must be taken into account: zoning requirements, required building setbacks, parking requirements, and any setbacks that relate to the parking. All these factors must be considered when developing the site design for your project and can have a drastic impact on the final layout for your office.

Ideally, the building should be oriented east/west on a given site, with the entry facing south and all the treatment rooms on the north side so that they get even, northern light through the windows. Practically speaking, this "perfect scenario" is seen about 40 percent of the time. Keep in mind, not every site will be perfect. A site may have a certain slope or drastic grade changes, and this could dictate where the building must be located. Or perhaps the best lot your team can locate is on the side of a street where the ops cannot face north. Don't lose heart; an experienced design team can still develop a high-functioning floor plan that accommodates the constraints of your chosen property.

It might seem obvious, but the building entry must be located in a way that makes it very clear that this is where to go to get in. There are a number of buildings that have confusing entries—avoid making it difficult for your patients to find your entry.

The location of your signage is also part of the site design. All signage—whether it's mounted on the building or is a free-standing sign—must adhere to local signage requirements, including how large it can be and where it can be located. Signage must be visible, legible, and attractive while conforming to the requirements of the governing municipality, association, or development covenants. Also, be sure to provide the maximum amount of signage allowed in your given area. The more visible your signage is, the better.

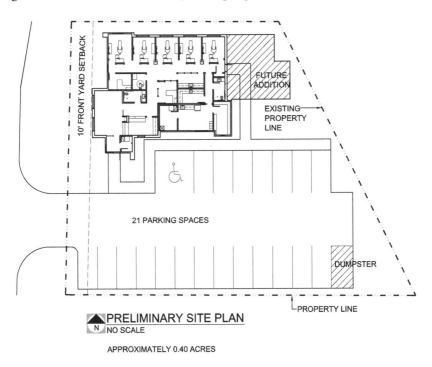

A conceptual site plan for a parcel of land one of our clients purchased. The treatment rooms face north, the preferred operatory orientation whenever feasible.

Vehicle access is also a very important consideration for the site design. The parking lot must be big enough and designed well for easy in and out. There must also be adequate access for handicapped parking near the main entry. Sometimes, the site is a really good choice except for the traffic access. One of our clients was considering a great site with good visibility on a main road in his town. The problem was that the road in front of the property had a center median. Only people coming from the east could turn directly into a parking lot. The rest would have to go out to the traffic light a block away, turn around, and come back. In the end, the doctor decided this restriction didn't make sense for his patients, and he chose another, more accessible site.

Site Design Steps

Once the site has been settled and the project is moving forward, most municipalities require that a licensed civil engineer perform civil engineering design for the property. The municipality must review and approve the design. At this point, you or your team must engage a local civil engineer to take the conceptual site plan and use it to create the civil engineering documents needed to obtain city approval for site construction. If any environmental or geotechnical testing (soil boring) is needed, it is usually performed around the time civil engineering begins—sometimes sooner if the property is suspected to have issues.

A site plan and the engineering documents are also needed if the subject property needs a zoning variance or rezoning request approved. Most places want to see what you're proposing in order to grant the request. The site design is also needed for all the other permits, variances, and approvals that are needed before work can begin. Even a small renovation project needs a building permit and probably also some other approvals from the municipality. In many cases, the bigger the project, the more the paperwork for things such as zoning variances and planning board presentations.

Architectural Floor Plan Development

The foundation of the architectural design process begins with an honest analysis of your current office practice (if you have one). Look around you. How does your office look and feel? What sort of impressions do patients form based on what they're seeing in your current office? How is the patient flow? Is the office outdated? Is it tired? Is it beat up? Is it clean and tidy but undersized? Are you missing areas you need for optimum efficiency? Sometimes an office looks nice and the practice is doing well, but the space is just undersized. The practice could really bloom in a bigger office with additional treatment rooms.

Even if you say, "I'm positive I want to do a brand-new office, no need to discuss it any further," your architect should see your current facility. It's helpful to get a sense of what you're used to and the environment that you're working in. Sometimes, for instance, a dentist says, "My waiting room is way too small." Maybe in this case the waiting room is actually a pretty good size, but the check-in area really needs improvement.

The objective of seeing your current office is to establish a baseline. From there, imagine what you want in the new place. In a perfect world, what would you have in the new office?

Frequently, the challenge is getting the owner-dentist to think beyond just modifying or tweaking the current space. Your space is what you're used to, but think beyond that. Open your mind and consider the possibilities of a new office as a blank canvas. Don't think of the design of the new facility based on the inherent limitations of your current office. Be open to exploring a layout and elements that are more efficient and conducive to good dentistry and making your patients feel welcome and comfortable. Think about your long-term aspirations for your practice as well. What should your new office have to help you achieve your goals?

Think about what you hate most about your current office and what you like best. What do you really wish you could change? What's working? What's not? What do your team members complain about? What do your patients complain about? What do they compliment you on? What would you change to attract a different type of clientele?

At the same time, be realistic based on your budget. As you move forward with the design phase, the primary job of your team should be to help keep your decisions in line with the budget. Maybe floor-to-ceiling glass on all four sides of the building would look really, really cool, and maybe your patients would really enjoy a big koi pond in your seating area, but if it's not going to work with your budget, you may not want to waste time going down those roads.

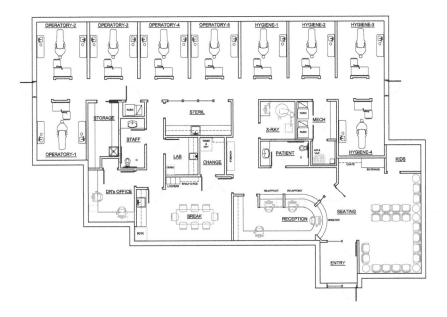

A sample floor plan for a nine operatory dental office.

For the interior of the office, give careful thought to your desires. Do you like your current color scheme? If it's mauve and green from 1989, maybe it's time for a more contemporary look. Do you like your current wood and wood tones, flooring materials, and your wall finishes? What about the lighting fixtures? The plumbing fixtures? During this phase of the design, you'll do a deep dive into flooring, lighting, finishes, trim styles, door styles—taking a comprehensive look at all the finishes on the inside of your office.

If you don't like what you have, what do you like? What do you hate? You can really narrow the options if you say, "Look, I don't know a whole lot, I just know I don't like oak or maple." Whether you realize it or not, you've now greatly narrowed your wood finish options and made the decisions going forward much easier.

It's important that the design of your office be "contextualized." That is, the look and feel both inside and out needs to be mindful of the area in which it's being built, as well as the perception it will likely evoke in the minds of your patients. An office in downtown Chicago is probably going to be catering to a lot of young professionals who enjoy the urban lifestyle. It's a safe bet that a modern office would have much more appeal in that context than an office in rural North Dakota in a town of 2,500 people. On the flip side, a rustic log cabin feel might not play well in a downtown Chicago setting but might appeal to a more rural clientele.

For example, we did a pediatric dental office in a lake town with a lot of vacation homes. A lot of the architecture in town has a lake house theme. To fit in with that, this dentist's waiting room has white wood beadboard, some stones that are reminiscent of the stones around the lake, and a couple of boat decorations. It's appropriate for the area, but it probably wouldn't be appropriate in Manhattan.

Of course, in many cases the budget comes into play for design decisions. Lots of times it's a process of give and take. You can spend a little bit more money here if you're willing to maybe not spend as much there. One of the things we always say is, "Spend money where it matters." You probably don't need granite countertops in your break room. You may very well want granite or quartz at the reception desk to create a positive impression for patients.

Spatial Relationships

Certain spatial relationships are critical for a dental office. Dental offices also have very specific infrastructure requirements that add time and cost to construction. This must be factored into the budget because infrastructure is an area where you can't cut any corners. Making sure the infrastructure conforms to national and local building codes is a crucial step at this point. Building something that turns out not to be up to code is quite expensive.

In terms of spatial relationships, there are three primary areas in a dental office that must be considered when developing your initial design: the administrative area, the clinical area, and the public area.

The administrative area includes the portions of your office intended primarily for staff or doctor use (not patient), including the break room, staff restroom, doctor's office(s), work room, and the mechanical room.

The clinical area includes the treatment rooms, operatories, and/or treatment bays, imaging room, sterilization, lab, and bulk storage.

The public area includes the front entry, seating area, reception area, consultation room(s), and the public restroom.

When developing the design of your dental office, it is important for your architect to know the dental office zones and be sure that elements of the same zone remain in close proximity. Having specific elements of a given zone in the inappropriate location can contribute to a less-than-efficient design.

For example, if your consultation room is located at the far end of the office in the treatment area (a long distance from the seating area), every time you use it for initial consultations you'll have to walk patients through the treatment area—a less-than-ideal situation. It will also make using this room with patients who have questions about their bill (and would prefer to talk privately) more difficult and less convenient. Ideally, the consultation room should be situated near the reception area so patients can quickly and easily be brought into the room for discussions.

A dental-specific architect will be familiar with the zones of a dental office and the appropriate adjacencies; rely on their expertise when developing your initial floor plan.

Site Design Impacts Long-Term Office Goals

We recently worked with a doctor in Minnesota that had been practicing for five years. He had purchased a practice and the four-operatory building that housed the practice from a retiring dentist. After about four years in the space, the doctor realized the office was too small. He came to us wanting to build an eight-operatory office. After a few weeks of looking at potential lots on which a new office could be built we settled on a .9-acre parcel about a mile from the existing office.

During the Vision Casting process the doctor indicated he would like to bring in an associate down the road, perhaps even two associates. Given this, the design of the office included the design of a 4-operatory addition that could be built at a later date should he determine it was necessary. However, the site presented some challenges that made exploring this option not without difficulty.

The lot sloped both front to back and side to side and included about ten feet of grade change for both directions it sloped. Given the contours of the lot, the most logical place to locate the water detention area happened to be right where the future addition should go. When we presented the facts to the doctor, he was discouraged, as he thought he would need to abandon the plans for the future addition. However, we shared with him another option that could address this situation.

If we filled in the area where the detention basin was initially planned, the site grades would then allow for the addition. If we did this, however, we would need to find another space on site for the detention area. Working with our civil engineer we came up with a solution that could contain the storm water in oversized concrete pipes under the parking area and behind the curb of the parking lot. This option was about $15,000 more expensive than the first option proposed. Ultimately, though, these modifications to the site design allowed the doctor to plan for the future addition he desired and not sacrifice anything related to the design of the office.

Chapter 6:

Developing the Floor Plan

The development of your floor plan begins with understanding your vision for the space. Talk with your architect about everything you like and don't like about the flow and layout of your current office (if you have one). This will help them develop a plan that aligns with your vision.

The waiting room and patient check-in/checkout areas are the first things a patient sees, so they need special attention. They must make an immediate good impression. When patients enter the building, it must be clear right away where to go, without confusion. The reception area should be visible at once. The patient should be able to head straight to it, without having to walk through the seating area or only a small portion of where other patients are seated.

Most practices with ten treatment rooms or fewer should size the greeter station part of the reception area for just one person because there's not usually a big influx or rush of people coming in all at once. One person can typically handle the check-in in these offices. Of course, larger offices may require more help at the check-in area. The checkout area, however, is different from the check-in area. This is a common bottleneck in practices, and typically your design should accommodate at least two people. In most cases, the check-in/checkout ratio should be 1:2.

The checkout area should provide some level of privacy—visible or aural, depending upon the circumstances—for your patients. This is where patients pay, and sometimes they need to have a discussion with the staff or the business manager about how to handle their bill or insurance. You don't want them to feel embarrassed talking about payment plans or issues with their dental insurance in front of everyone in the waiting area. Ideally, there should be a good level of visual privacy at the checkout area. The checkout stations can be subdivided using full-height walls, partial-height walls, or glass to give visual separation if multiple people are checking out at the same time.

Aural privacy is a bit more difficult to accommodate, but the distance from the seating area can help achieve this to some degree. Placing the seating area as far away from the checkout area as possible provides good separation between patients in the seating area and patients paying their bill. Coat racks, beverage counters, a wall and a door, and other types of dividers can help create separation between the seating and the checkout area.

Some offices elect to have a consultation room adjacent the checkout area that can be used for both treatment consultations with the doctor as well as financial consultations with the office manager. If a client is checking out and there's an issue with the bill, instead of having a conversation up at the reception area, the client can be guided to the consultation room for privacy behind a closed door. The consultation room should ideally have two entries, one for the patient and one for the staff member. Consider using lots of glass in the doors and walls of this room so the patient feels comfortable in what is typically a small office.

The look of the seating area depends on what you desire. It generally should match the rest of the office appearance in terms of look and feel. Some doctors want a very modern look, while others prefer a homier feel. No matter what the style, the same basic considerations spelled out below apply.

A seating and reception area with dedicated kids area (left), consultation room with textured glass (center), work room (center-right) and beverage station (far right).

Many doctors like to put in a beverage station for the convenience of the patients (and also staff). Some offices provide a coffee machine, hot water, bottled water, and other bottled drinks. Many doctors want a TV in the waiting room, but this is a personal preference issue. This gives people something to watch, but it also gives the doctor a marketing opportunity. You can run intermittent commercials, patient education videos, or a loop of the services you can provide.

The majority of offices do something for kids in the seating area, even if it's just having some kids' books on display. Many set up a dedicated children's area in a corner of the waiting area or an alcove or even another room if there's enough space in your floor plan. A doctor with a lot of younger patients will obviously want to do more than one who primarily treats adults.

Some offices choose to put a fireplace in the waiting room. In most cases, they're not the working kind—they don't even burn gas—but they give the space a nice, relaxing feel. They make patients feel more comfortable. Others opt for a fish tank or a water feature to create interest in the seating area.

The type of seating in the waiting area is, again, a personal choice. It should be commercial grade, as over time this seating will get lots of use. As a rule of thumb, the minimum number of seats in the seating area should be 1.25 to 2 times the number of treatment rooms. In rural areas, you may need more seating. In many cases, people in rural areas may be in town running multiple errands, and oftentimes these families bring more people with them to their appointment. In rural areas, 2.5 times to 3 times the number of treatment rooms may be more appropriate. For more variety in the space, some doctors end up with a mixture of sofas and individual chairs. A bariatric seat to accommodate heavy patients is another item you may want to consider for your seating area.

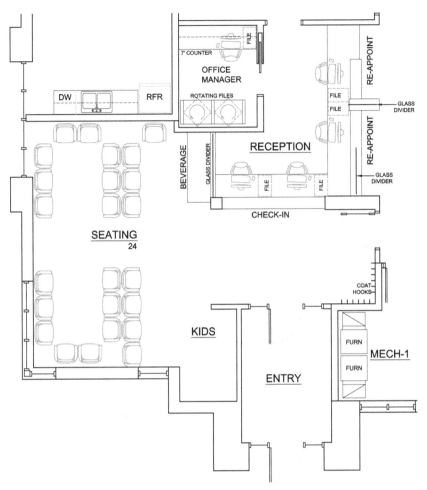

A portion of a floor plan showing the following spaces: reception, office manager's office, seating area, entry, and kids area. The spaces in this plan are sized appropriately for this particular office and have correct adjacencies for most practices.

A patient restroom should be located somewhere near the patient seating area. Many doctors choose to locate the patient restroom outside the seating area, unless it's a lease building with restrooms in the common area of the building. An optimal place to locate the public restrooms is behind the door leading into the clinical area. Since it is right by the reception area, your staff can keep an eye on

97

things better than if it is located in the seating area. If a young child or an elderly or handicapped person is using the restroom, your staff can also provide assistance, if necessary. The reception area staff can also easily check on the restroom all day long to be certain it's clean and ready to use. If the restroom is far away from the front desk or directly off the seating area, your staff cannot see it as well and may forget to monitor it.

As silly as it may sound, how clean and attractive the patient restroom is plays a big part in how patients judge your office. Again, this is a chance to make a good impression. This is an area to spend money generously to make the restroom as nice as possible. It's not uncommon to see quartz or granite countertops, ceramic tile floors, ceramic tile wainscot and accents, high-end light fixtures, and other quality finishes that really make an impact in this room.

In a larger, multi-tenant building, the restrooms may be in the common area. In these situations, you don't have any control over them, which can be a problem if the building maintenance isn't as good as it should be. When doing a lease build-out, many owner-dentists elect to still build in a staff and/or patient restroom within their suite. This adds to the expense of the build-out, but it is definitely worthwhile. It's more convenient for everybody not to have to leave the office and go down the hall to use the restrooms. It also gives you much more control over how the restroom looks and the impression it makes.

Just about every doctor will want a personal office in the space. The size depends on the individual. You won't spend much time there, so you don't necessarily want or need a large space. But some doctors use their office more than others, and some want to display memorabilia or other items there, so they want something bigger. It's generally agreed that you don't make a lot of money sitting in your office, so there's probably some wisdom in having it be modestly sized.

A private doctor's office, a comfortable space that showcases some of the doctor's personal interests.

Most small dental practices don't have a full-time office manager. Once a practice gets above six to seven operatories, however, many doctors have someone on staff to handle administration. If there's enough work for the practice to hire a dedicated office manager, some offices prefer to move that person out from the reception area and into a dedicated workspace. Ideally, the space will overlook or be in close proximity to the reception area so the office manager can see people as they check in and out and be on hand to easily help with overflow, answer questions, take patients to the consultation area if they need to discuss anything in private, and generally keep an eye on things. For bigger practices, a back office area for a bookkeeper, insurance specialist, or marketing person is something to consider including in your plan.

Dental-Specific Space Requirements in Your Floor Plan

Now let's discuss the dental-specific elements of your floor plan. It's crucial to make sure the design of the clinical area is done correctly. One key to an efficient layout is centrally locating the sterilization center. All the treatment rooms need to be supplied with sterilized tools (either a tray or cassette they're using). When the treatment is complete, the tools need to be returned and sterilized quickly so they can be processed and be put back into service for procedures. Because of this constant back and forth, the shorter the distance your team has to travel, the more efficient the office can be. Your staff will visit this room more often than any other room in your office on any given day and, over the course of a day, saving a few steps here and there can really add up! If the sterilization area isn't centrally located, a lot of time and energy is wasted.

If you have an office with five or six treatment rooms, the sterilization area doesn't need to be huge—generally 1.5 to 2.5 lineal feet of counter top per treatment room. If additional growth is planned (building addition or expansion of the space), however, you likely want to make the sterilization area larger than might be needed right away. The circulation space in the center area needs to flow well. The larger the office, the more people are going to be accessing the space at the same time. Some people will be working in the sterilization area while others are coming in and dropping off their used instruments and picking up new instruments. You don't want this area to become a bottleneck, as is often the case in dental offices.

In most cases it's appropriate to start the floor plan development process by putting the sterilization area in a pod in the center of the building. Locating the bulk supply closet immediately adjacent to sterilization is strongly suggested, as again, your team will need items from it many times during the day. Your imaging room should also be in the central pod or as close to it as possible, so you can easily take patients to it on their way to the treatment area.

An L-shaped sterilization center. The red lighted cabinet is designated for dirty items, and the blue lighted area is where sterilized cassettes are placed.

What is outlined above is the most efficient approach for designing the central core of your office. An experienced dental-specific architect can adhere to these principles in just about any space. Do not compromise efficiencies when having your plan developed—you and your team will regret it down the road.

The typical treatment room in a general dental practice today is 10'6" wide by 11'6" deep. The final dimensions of your treatment rooms will depend on the style and configuration of the dental cabinetry and delivery equipment you select for your office. If you chose an operatory configuration with no side cabinets, for example, room widths can typically be reduced to 8'6" wide.

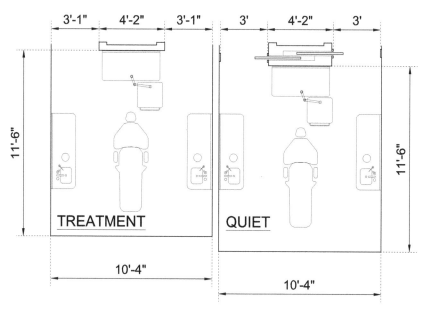

Two standard general dentist treatment room designs. The room on the right shows an expanded headwall detail with dual pocket doors, used in cases where a quiet operatory is desired.

Openings into the treatment rooms include doorways, doors, and clear space between cabinetry. The primary opening must maintain 32" clear width in order to accommodate handicap accessibility. The secondary access into a treatment room does not need to meet this standard. The preferred width is 36" wide. Some offices elect to provide doors on some (or all) of the treatment rooms. To accommodate ADA requirements, these doors must either be surface mounted on the exterior of room (barn door style) or recessed as pocket doors. If a traditional swing door is desired, the room orientation of the room must flip 90 or 180 degrees, placing the 12 o'clock cabinet on the opposite side of the room from the doors.

The head wall of the treatment room is another design consideration to keep in mind. A freestanding dental cabinet can be used at the head wall, or a wall can be constructed to which a cabinet is affixed or recessed. The design and depth of the head wall impacts the treatment room and hallway dimensions—be certain this is considered when designing the treatment rooms.

Two examples of corridor headwalls. The design options are nearly limitless, and can include wood trim, sconces, and vinyl wall coverings.

Two additional examples of corridor headwalls. These designs include wood trim, sconces, modularArts (above), stone, accent paint, and a free-standing dental cabinet (below).

When designing the treatment rooms, something else to consider is whether you're planning to bring a specialist into your office. In some markets, a general dentist might want an endodontist (or other specialist) to come in and treat patients a day or two a week. If this is a consideration, you'll want to design the operatories to accommodate this.

Room sizes for specialist practices are typically different from general dental treatment rooms. Oral surgery suites, for instance, are larger in both depth and width to accommodate patient, doctor, and assistant movement, as well as the necessary surgical equipment. Open bays, common for both orthodontists and pediatric dentists, must be more concerned with the spacing of the chairs and the location of the cabinetry or carts required for procedures. They must also determine if and how they want to provide private or semi-private treatment areas, whether by partitioning off a portion of the open bay or inside individual rooms.

An orthodontic treatment area, including two semi-private treatment chairs at opposing ends of the open bay.

The efficient design of several important areas in a dental office is key to efficiency, quick room turnaround, avoiding bottlenecks, and minimizing fatigue.

Oftentimes the larger the office in terms of treatment rooms, the larger the sterilization area needs to be; a bigger office also needs more storage space for all the procedural supplies. The storage area should be sized based on how busy the practice is and how many treatment rooms there are.

The size of the lab area depends on how much work you do in-house versus how much gets sent to an outside lab. That's a very individual and depends in part on the type of practice. In some cases, the lab only needs four or five feet of countertop. Other labs easily need double or triple that to have enough room for all the equipment. Today, some dentists have a CEREC or an E4D for making inlays, crowns, onlays, and veneers. Some doctors want the milling machine in the lab area, while others actually have the machine on display in a patient corridor or alcove.

A display alcove to highlight a CEREC used in this dental office.

Mistakes in locating these areas lead to inefficient operations and long room turnaround times. Mistakes in sizing the spaces lead to areas that can't grow with the practice. And mistakes in the infrastructure lead to costly reworking and downtime. These are areas where an inexperienced designer can badly miscalculate.

Many doctors want to have nitrous oxide available. If the nitrous oxide lines are piped to the operatories—as opposed to being delivered from a cart—this can be complicated from an infrastructure standpoint. The tanks should be located near an exit if at all possible to make it easier to get them in and out. The room that holds the tanks must be fire-rated, and this requires very specific venting requirements to keep the fire risk to a minimum. This is another case where the architect needs a lot of experience, both to know the requirements and how to meet them in a cost-effective way.

Just as the sterilization area is the heart of the treatment space, the mechanical room, where the dental compressor, dental vacuum, and in some cases HVAC units go, is the heart of the infrastructure. Your design must find a way to accommodate this room. If the new office is in a leased space, one of the first things we need to discover is where the heating and air-conditioning units are located. If they're not on the building rooftop or cannot be located there, floor space must be provided for them. In a new building, either location can make sense depending upon the style of building being built. The size of your office will drive the size and number of mechanical rooms necessary. As previously stated, the air compressor and vacuum pump are both very loud pieces of equipment. Ideally, they should be located as far away from the treatment rooms and waiting areas as possible.

Because employees spend some of their downtime in the break room, having this space as roomy and comfortable as practically possible is a good idea for staff morale. Oftentimes, the break room will include a sink, dishwasher, and a microwave. The break room often also doubles as an area where the team can have its stand-up meeting or "huddle" in the morning. Often it is also where continuing education for the staff happens, so some doctors want a TV and want to make sure there's enough room to bring in some extra chairs.

Code Requirements and Infrastructure Design

Your architect and other design team professionals must follow both local and national building codes and also be aware of ways in which municipalities can have their own additional ordinances. For example, some cities require a urinal in each single-user restroom for men. This is not in case in every city, and it is one of hundreds of items that must be verified when developing your design. Your design team should work with local authorities to make certain the plans meet the specific requirements for that municipality. You want to discover these wrinkles before getting too far along in the design process.

Plumbing is really important in a dental office. Most treatment rooms have a sink, as do the sterilization area and the lab. Relative to a general office space, this is a lot of plumbing. In addition to the plumbing, each treatment room needs vacuum lines and compressed air lines, as do the sterilization area and the lab. Some offices choose to run medical gas lines for nitrous oxide. Many offices ask for a natural gas line installed to the lab or sterilization room. Every treatment room, imaging area, sterilization area, and lab also needs specialized electrical lines.

A dental office could need as many as six types of plumbing lines, all with very specific requirements. The drain lines and vacuum lines typically should go under the floor. The water lines often go under the floor, but they can come from overhead if needed. The compressed air lines can run overhead. The natural gas line runs overhead as well.

The water lines generally connect to the main line from the municipality. If the water needs treatment (hard water is really, really bad for dental equipment), sometimes a water softener system must be installed. Many offices install a recirculation pump so that the hot water comes out right away, as opposed to waiting 10–20 seconds after the tap is turned on for water.

The air compressor and vacuum pump are both very loud pieces of equipment. Whenever possible, they should be located in a mechanical room away from the treatment areas and waiting areas. To help keep the noise level down, these items can be located in a separate, soundproofed room within a room. If the constraints of the space prevent this from being done, the walls of mechanical room can be built out of masonry block because masonry is great for sound attenuation. Over this wall, a standard wall can be built with additional sound insulation. This double design wall helps minimize noise from the compressor and vacuum.

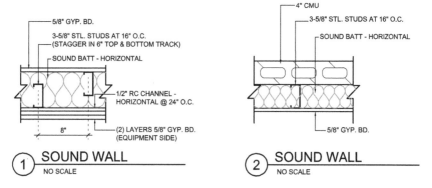

Two different sound wall details used to mitigate noise coming from the mechanical room of a dental office.

Electrical lines for a dental office must be powered correctly to accommodate the latest technology and specialized equipment, such as lasers, sterilizers, and digital X-ray units. These items need careful attention in the design to make sure there's enough power and that the system meets the code for medical-grade electrical requirements. National standards should be followed, but sometimes municipalities have their own additional ordinances that are stricter.

In the treatment room, the number-one priority is getting correct wiring to the twelve o'clock cabinet, the chair, and/or the twoside cabinets. The equipment you're going to have and its location must be discussed with you your dental equipment representative in great detail. This will ensure the installation of appropriate electrical outlets, whips, conduits, and data ports. Today's dental office is much more IT intensive than it was ten or fifteen years ago, so you also must consider the locations of the computers and monitors in the operatories and make sure there are adequate lines to run power and data to them. Your office will require dedicated circuits for all the important equipment like the X-ray machine and the sterilization equipment so that if one circuit gets tripped, other parts of the office don't lose power.

Treatment Room Lighting

In the treatment room, the lighting that matters most to the patient is the dental light above the chair. These can vary quite a bit, so be sure to give this item careful consideration. The type of bulb varies in these lights, and right now the trend is toward LED fixtures. This may change over time to something even more efficient.

The dental light fixture is typically on an articulating arm, but where to mount it is something for you to decide. In many cases, they're mounted on the ceiling with an articulating arm mount. Alternatively, they can be mounted on a track connected to the ceiling. The light moves back and forth along the track and still has an articulating arm. It can also be wall-mounted by connecting it to the wall on one side of the chair. It can also be mounted to the dental chair. Finally, the dental light can be installed on top of a wall cabinet or shared center cabinets. The advantage to the wall mount and wall cabinet/shared center cabinet mount location is that the light can be moved out of the way entirely and pushed flat against the wall, whereas the ceiling mounted options are, to some degree, mildly in the way for a small portion of the room.

Another lighting factor to consider is the balance of artificial and natural light in the treatment rooms. This is something to be mindful of because the environment in the operatory should help reduce unnecessary fatigue for you. During dental procedures, you're shining a very bright light into a dark mouth. That makes the pupils in your eyes contract. Looking up from the mouth into a room that's poorly lit makes your pupils dilate to let in more light. Switching back and forth between the bright light in the mouth and dim light in the room is fatiguing for your eyes. The treatment room should be well lit, with even illumination.

The orientation of your building on the site plays a big part in the role natural light plays in your operatories. As previously stated, your building cannot always be perfectly oriented relative to the direction of the sunlight. A northern or eastern orientation is desirable. To help control sunlight, use perforated shades on windows. Sometimes including larger overhangs on the building will further help reduce the sunlight coming into the clinical areas.

The ceiling fixtures in the treatment rooms need to provide even coverage for the room at a good illumination level. They also need to be in the right color temperature range. This is crucial for the doctor when it comes to color matching fillings, veneers, and so forth. The light in the room should be similar to normal daylight. To get that same light indoors, use bulbs that are at 4,000 degrees Kelvin. The higher the temperature, the whiter the light is and the closer it is to natural daylight. Color temperatures over 5,000 K start to have a blue cast to them. Color temperatures below 3,000 K can have a yellowish cast.

Many light fixtures in treatment rooms are 2 x 4 troughs that use a fluorescent bulb. This is an easy way to ensure the right color temperature. LED bulbs come in various color temperatures as well. Again, these are becoming more popular. As with fluorescent lights, LED bulbs need to be the right color temperature.

Exterior Design Considerations

The look and feel of the exterior of your building also plays a big part in the impression your patients form about you and your practice. When remodeling a building or building a new building, there are dozens of styles (i.e., traditional, contemporary, prairie-style, mid-century) and material options (i.e., brick, limestone, composite metal panel, vinyl siding, EIFS) to consider—too many to contemplate in this book. The exterior look of your building is a matter of personal taste, but it's important to remember that the exterior design of your building should be developed with the goal of making a positive impression on your patients.

In instances where you are leasing an existing building, there may be little if anything you can do to change the exterior look of the building. In these cases it's important to select a building that makes a positive impression—one that appears clean, up to date, and well maintained. Consider things such as the condition of the parking areas, the landscaping, and the signage. A well-kept building exterior will reinforce what patients see when they walk through the doors of your office.

The exterior of a dental office, including brick, limestone, aluminum frames and glass and a metal roof.

In some locations municipal design standards or restrictive covenants tied to the property may dictate what your building must look like. These requirements may call for a certain percentage of your building to be masonry or glass or may require a specific style of roof or façade. In some cases, the city or the party selling the land may require the exterior design be reviewed and approved before you can begin construction. It's important to know if such requirements exist in a given area and be sure design a building that complies with the standards on the front end—this will save time and money later.

Visioning a Future Practice

When we sit down with a dentist to think about their future practice, we start by talking about the current office. A recent example is a doctor who bought a practice from a retiring doctor but initially decided against also buying the building. Instead, she rented it from the retired doctor. The building was from the 1950s, and had eight-foot ceilings. It was originally set up to accommodate two different dentists, but this doctor was a solo practitioner. This led to a very confusing situation for patients because when they walked in the door, there were literally two seating areas. Patients could go either to the right or the left. The best this doctor could do about the confusion was to put up a sign saying, "Please see the receptionist to the left."

The office was outdated and inefficient. Just as it had two seating areas, it also had two sterilization areas. The whole space was very cramped. Clearly, something had to be done, but the doctor needed our guidance to figure out what.

When we started talking, she wondered if it would make sense to buy the building and remodel it to suit her needs. As we talked about her dream office, she made it clear very early on that, in a perfect world, she didn't want to deal with owning a building. She preferred to just be a tenant. We also discussed with her what she wanted in an office. At the top of her list was lots of natural light, which her current office didn't have at all.

She wanted a space with ten-foot ceilings so that the office felt more open. She also wanted something that was more in line with her style. She wanted a space that was warm and inviting, with darker woods and a fireplace. She wanted the office to be a place that felt comfortable to her and her patients. She also needed more parking and better access to her building—her current location had an undersized parking lot and a driveway that was difficult to get in and out of.

We spent a fair amount of time talking about her current office to see if we could achieve what she was seeking in the current building. We developed a concept plan that addressed many of the ills of the current floor plan, then put together costs associated with doing a renovation of her current office. We also evaluated historical cost data of new construction build-outs and provided this information to her so she could compare the two options. In her case, it ended up being about 15 percent less to do a renovation of her current building than to go to build out a new lease space elsewhere.

Ultimately, when we found some spaces that were available to lease, she started to see how moving could give her the opportunity to have a nicer, more open space with things she wanted, like lots of windows and good parking. Moving would create some disruption, but it would be a lot less than the disruption of a big renovation.

The seating and reception area of the new office, including an electric fireplace (left) and a beverage counter (right).

The space she chose had nearly everything on her wish list: good parking, high ceilings, and good natural light. It was also in a high-growth area of town, an improvement over her current location. She was currently in a more established area of town, but most of the buildings around her were older and showing their age.

The new space was unfinished—a blank canvas for her. We were able to incorporate ten-foot ceilings, and she was able to get her fireplace and lots of windows. She was able to achieve everything she was looking for in a new office. From the time we sat down to have that first serious visioning talk to the time she opened the doors of her new office was about nine months.

At the start, she was very hesitant to proceed. She was concerned about how much of her time the project would take. Because we handle so much of the work, including finding a new location and conducting the negotiations for it, she didn't have to put in that many extra hours to get the office of her dreams. As she told me, "When I told my friends about what I was doing, they all said, 'Oh, you must be crazy-busy and super-stressed.' But you guys just made it easy. I didn't feel stressed. I didn't feel crazy."

Chapter 7:

Interior Design

The interior design of a dental office is an extremely important part of patient and employee satisfaction—and your satisfaction as well. This is an area where an interior designer without experience in dental office design can make many expensive, time-consuming mistakes. Working with an experienced firm helps you get an attractive, personalized, and cost-effective interior design scheme right from the start.

Imagining Your New Office

Although the discussion of plan and building design is separate from interior design in this book, the two cannot practically be separated. During the development of your floor plan, your architect is already contemplating the interior design elements of your office. Selections made in the interior design phase are often a reflection of what was originally envisioned and discussed during plan development. The convergence of these two elements yields what is necessary to create your architectural plans.

As with the architectural design process, interior design begins with an understanding of your vision. Work with your design team to select interior design elements and finishes that work well for your office and also reflect your personal likes and dislikes. Consider the following:

- What should the waiting room and patient checkout area look like?
- What would you want patients to say about your office?
- How do you want to set your practice apart from other practices in the area?
- What are your personal preferences for your work space (natural light, high ceilings, noise levels, etc.)?
- What are your personal style preferences (modern, industrial, colonial, muted or vivid colors, curtains or blinds, etc.)?

A bold use of accent colors set against the white solid surface reception desk creates a striking visual impact in this reception area.

In all these decisions, you and your design team are after some combination of durability, hygiene, appearance, and cost. Sometimes one factor ends up being the most important. For one office we did recently, cost was ruling the project. For parts of the office, the client chose flooring that isn't as durable and easy to maintain as we would like to see. Over time, it will need to be replaced. Keeping costs down let this project get off the ground, however, so at the time that was the best option. When the time comes, the client expects the office will be profitable and plans to replace the flooring with something more durable.

The inverse of that scenario is often the case, however. You may not want to have to deal with maintenance. You may want all your chosen materials to last a long time. You may be willing to spend more for low-maintenance or maintenance-free products that look good and wear well.

One factor to consider is how long you plan to be in the office. If you only plan to stay five years, then durability isn't that big of a consideration, and some costs may go down. But if you plan to be there for a long time, quality and durability become the main requirements. You don't want to have the trouble and expense of replacing the floors and counters every five to seven years.

Paints and Finishes

The best color choices for a dental office are whatever colors you prefer. A pediatric dentist might want brighter colors, but this isn't always the case. Some pediatric dentists want cartoon themes, and others want more of a spa feel for the parents. The question in that case is, are you designing it for the kids or for the parents?

Your design team will work with you to get a feel for your color preferences. From there a specific color palette is developed. For many offices, the palette usually ends with three to five colors, with one major field color and then accent colors as appropriate. Wall finishes generally come down to a combination of vinyl wall covering and paint. Vinyl wall covering is low-maintenance and is extremely durable, so it's an excellent choice. Some offices desire wainscoting or wall coverings for high-traffic areas, such as the seating area, patient corridors, and even the treatment rooms. In other areas it may make sense to opt for vinyl wall covering on the bottom portion of a wall and paint on top, divided by a chair rail.

Countertops and Cabinetry

The possibilities for countertops and cabinetry in the office are almost endless. Begin to narrow down your choices looking at appearance, cost, and how the colors fit into the overall color palette that's been chosen. Quartz countertops, for instance, are a man-made material that uses about 95 percent natural quartz held together with a binding agent. Quartz functions very much like granite. It's just as hard, but you can control the look and make the countertop appear more uniform. Granite is an all-natural material, but every slab has a slightly different look. The benefit of quartz is that you have more control over the final appearance. When cost is more of a consideration, we recommend a solid surface such as Corian. Laminate is an even less expensive alternative. As always, we have to balance cost against durability and appearance. Consider having soft-close hinges and soft-close drawers in all the cabinetry of your office. It's a relatively cost-effective way to reduce noise in the office. Nobody likes to hear banging drawers or doors all day long!

In many situations, it's in the best interest of the doctor to purchase dental cabinetry from a dental equipment manufacturer for the treatment rooms and sterilization center of their office. These cabinets are extremely durable and are typically assembled in a factory with rigid quality standards. There's also a high degree of integration with the dental delivery system and the cabinetry, especially if using delivery from the 12 o'clock cabinet or side cabinet. Finally, there are significant tax advantages that come from purchasing what can be considered a piece of dental equipment, as opposed to something custom built into the office. The balance of the non-dental cabinetry finishes and hardware for your office can be selected to match or complement the dental manufacturer's offerings so the cabinetry ties together.

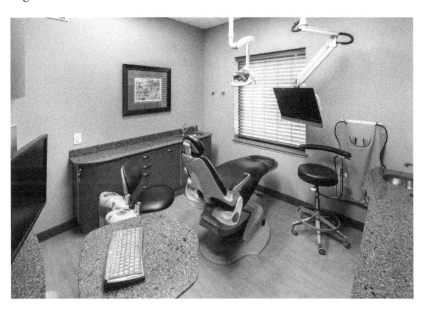

A treatment room with dental cabinetry, chair, light, monitors, and delivery unit.

Flooring

For the clinical areas of your office, we suggest hospital-grade anti-microbial flooring material. If your budget allows, luxury vinyl tile flooring or a similar product is preferable to vinyl composition tile. The luxury tiles come in a wide variety of finishes. Some doctors choose simulated wood-look because it gives a warm feel. A great advantage of the luxury vinyl tile is that it is low maintenance and wears well—much better than the composition tile. VCT must be stripped and waxed periodically—something that's inconvenient and disruptive to the practice, in addition to the cost.

Vinyl flooring comes in tiles, but the wood-look vinyl actually comes in planks, just like real wood. It has the same random grain as wood and gets installed in strips like wood. It's an excellent product that's very popular. Many manufacturers make high-quality vinyl flooring—there are many options.

An appropriate commercial-grade carpet will wear really well and should only need cleaning once or twice a year. Because carpet helps muffle noise, consider using it in the seating area, reception, patient corridors, imaging room, doctor's office, consultation room, and other non-treatment areas. For the entry vestibule or the entry area, in many cases we recommend walk-off carpet or a ceramic tile with an aluminum track/carpet insert. Walk-off carpet is specifically designed to knock off snow, water, mud, sand, salt, and so on from footwear as people enter the office. The carpet catches it—all you have to do is vacuum it up after the office closes. Instead of putting down mats, which are unattractive and can also be a trip hazard, walk-off carpet or a recessed track is a great solution for keeping the office looking beautiful.

A reception and seating area with "walk-off" carpet (in front of reception desk) and commercial grade carpet tiles (seating area) including colored accent carpet that mirrors the shape and contour of the ceiling soffits.

Windows and Window Treatments

Many offices are designed with non-operable windows. There are a lot of good reasons for this. A window left open overnight or on a weekend can let in the elements, especially from a bad rainstorm. That's not good for expensive dental equipment. Open windows also leave the office more vulnerable to a break-in. The cooling factor also must be considered. A dental office gets hot quickly from all the people, lights, and equipment. Opening the windows doesn't really help cool anything off most of the time, but it does let in the rain, snow, dust, air pollution, and a lot of noise. And in many places around the country, the air-conditioning is running in the office for at least eight or nine months of the year. In warmer places, it runs year-round. Non-operable windows are preferable as a way to reduce

125

street noise and keep the office temperature steady at a comfortable level throughout the year.

The type and color of window frame depends on the look of your building. Is it a more commercial look? A modern look? Residential? For the best temperature control, use double-paned windows made with low-emissive (low-E) glass. This is a clear window that has an invisible metal or metallic oxide coating. The coating reflects heat from sunlight but allows light to pass through. Low-E coatings help reduce energy consumption. The next step up is tinted windows; the next step after that is a reflective or mirror-type finish. The window glass is like the paint colors for the building—it comes down to personal preference.

The window treatments can be whatever you want that fits in with the rest of the design. Many offices use some type of mesh roller shade. These are modern, efficient, and last a long time. They cut down the solar gain to a surprising degree, anywhere from 93 to 99 percent, which makes the air-conditioning much more efficient. If you're standing inside the office, you can still look out with the shade pulled down, but it's virtually impossible to see into the office from the outside, so they also help with privacy.

Doors

Doors are an important design element, so choices must be made. Should the door be flat panel, flush, or raised panel? Should it be a three-panel, six-panel, or five-panel door? Should it have glass in it? The main goal is for the doors to fit well into the overall décor.

Solid core doors are the best for dental offices where noise levels are a concern. Barn-style doors or pocket doors can be good options depending on their location and use. The type of door used in your office will vary depending on where it is in the office. You may want the doors to the operatories, for instance, to have some glass so that activity in the room can be easily observed. The door to restroom should be solid and have no glass installed (for obvious reasons)!

Lighting

In addition to the specialized lighting in the operatories, you must consider general and task lighting in the rest of the office. The decorative lighting in the reception area, seating area, corridors, and other spaces (consultation room, for instance) is often overlooked. This lighting is important to the overall look and feel of the office. In an entryway, it's nice to have hanging pendant lights, especially if the entry is taller. Elsewhere, the lighting becomes part of the architectural design. Decorative sconces often work well in corridors. The lighting in the non-clinical portions of the office should be bright enough to illuminate the areas evenly.

For general lighting in the back room office areas, many offices use the same 2 x 4 ceiling fixtures that are in the treatment rooms so that the style ties together. The lighting is part of the overall feel of the office, so a lot depends on your personal taste.

Specialty Items

Many owner-dentists want to take their dental office design to the next level by adding specialty items to the waiting area. Specialty items add some personality to the office—they incorporate a little wow that makes the patient experience less stressful and maybe even fun.

Specialty items don't have to be over the top or crazy. The idea is to do something that conveys who you are, what you like, or what's important to you. Use specialty items to create an environment that's interesting and comfortable for the patient while simultaneously conveying a professional, clinically competent image. A fireplace is a great way to do this. It's inviting and comforting. Some dentists like to have a big fish tank. The fish are interesting to watch and are said to relax people. The tank can be any size you want, within the space limits.

Water features like small fountains are also very popular. They're calming to listen to, they cover up other noises, and they're enjoyable to watch. Installing them on the wall or floor is usually not a problem.

For a pediatric dental office, specialty items are almost a must. Most doctors in this practice area will spend a fair amount of money to make a great waiting area for the kids. They go way beyond just a Lego table and some kids' books. Other kid-friendly design elements include built-in video game consoles, climbing walls, and play areas with a slide.

A sports themed pediatric dental office seating area. A slide, small reading counter, and two video gaming stations are in the adjacent room through the door shown in the photo.

To add interest to the walls and also to make dividers of various sorts, offices can incorporate decorative acrylic, glass, or plaster panels as design elements. The panels are really great for adding texture and light to the architectural design. Where appropriate, these types of panels can be used instead of walls. For example, in an open dental office, panels can divide the chairs in the open bay while still keeping the open feel and letting in a lot of light. We recently used panels in a pediatric dental office to divide the kids' play area from the balance of the seating area. They make the area fun and different. These panels can be used in a wide variety of ways, from lighting to reception desks to dividing panels. When using these acrylic panels, it's mostly for accent and emphasis. Put them in the right place, and a little bit goes a long way.

Products from manufacturers such as 3Form and modularArts are available in two different types: panels, which can go into a wall or be attached to a wall, and blocks, which are larger and more three-dimensional. Every panel is unique. They're a lot of fun to use because they're very attractive and distinct. They give an office more design options, while also providing a nice contemporary feel.

Ceilings

Ceilings are another area that dentists don't typically think about until it's brought to their attention. There are a lot of types and styles. We base our recommendations mostly on the dentist's personal taste and the project budget, but other considerations come into play. Suggestions for a lease space, for instance, would depend on the height of the ceilings. If the office space is pretty standard, acoustical tiles for the ceiling are often suggested to cut down on noise.

Some spaces have tall ceilings. For instance, old warehouse buildings can have ceilings that are fifteen feet or higher—which are very high compared to standard nine-foot or ten-foot ceilings. Sometimes doctors prefer a lower, more standard ceiling height, and in buildings with a taller structure many times a drop ceiling is installed. Some doctors like the height for the open feeling it creates, but they want to see a standard ceiling, not all the "ugly" stuff that's usually covered by it. Others take the opposite approach. A lot of offices take advantage of the extra ceiling height to create a more interesting space by removing the ceiling to expose the beams, ductwork, and so on. The exposed structure can be painted in a range of interesting and fun ways, or you can install floating soffits or painted structures or just leave it as-is. The ceiling should match the overall feel of the office.

Curved, perforated metal panels provide visual interest to the corridor of this dental office and reiterate the curved elements of the design.

Art on the walls is the finishing touch for an office. Art should be chosen based on the style and feel of the office or what is in line with the doctor's personal taste. A lot of doctors have personal collections of art, collector's items, memorabilia, and the like that they want to display in the office. One of our dentists had a collection of St. Louis Cardinals memorabilia that meant a lot to him. Our design team created niches in the waiting area, the consultation room, and his personal office to display the memorabilia with lighting to accent the items. A lot of dentists also want a display area in the waiting area or reception area to highlight their community and charitable activities. Creating a wall space to show off pictures of such things is common in many offices.

Chapter 8:

Putting It All Together

Renovating, expanding, or moving a dental practice is a complex process. The help of your team, including those with professional design and construction expertise, will ensure a successful project. Professional help beginning early in the process makes the difference between a project that goes smoothly and stays within budget and one that goes badly and wastes a lot of your time and money.

Getting Construction Underway

Once the architectural plans and engineering drawings are complete, the next steps include submitting the paperwork for a building permit and putting the project out for bid. These are extremely important steps that need to be done correctly to avoid major delays and unexpected expenses later in the construction process.

Permitting

Arranging for all the permits necessary to get started on the construction, whether a ground-up project, an addition, or a large renovation, is complex. To avoid delays, the paperwork must be thoroughly prepared. The permitting process varies from municipality to municipality, but it generally takes three to four weeks for all the approvals to be granted. If the site plan must also be reviewed and approved, this process can take anywhere from four to twelve weeks. To avoid delay in cases where a site plan review and approval is necessary, the drawings must be submitted for approval in advance of the paperwork for the construction permit.

The required paperwork for the construction permit varies somewhat from place to place, but it almost always must include:
- Stamped architectural plans
- Civil engineering drawings (for ground-up buildings or building additions)
- Engineered mechanical, electrical, and plumbing drawings
- Energy code compliance documents
- 3-D exterior renderings of the building

Construction delays can be very, very expensive, so it's crucial to make sure that all the permitting documents are correct and submitted on time.

Pricing

Two different approaches can be used for pricing the project: hard bid (also called competitive bid) or negotiated bid. Understanding the differences will help you decide which approach to take.

In the hard bid approach, the general contractor or construction manager is selected solely on the basis of price. The lowest bid wins the project. This may seem like a good way to get the best overall price, but it usually isn't. The general contractor's fee is buried in the project costs—you can't tell what the fee actually is. And a general contractor will only build what's in the drawings. Any deviation from the original drawings will trigger a change order, which is billed to the client. In our experience, in hard-bid projects, many general contractors use a change order as a way to generate additional profit, so they have no incentive to try to avoid them. In a hard bid job, change orders typically add 20 percent or more to the overall project cost.

Hard bid contractors have every incentive to keep construction costs down, which is generally a good thing, but that also tempts them to use the cheapest materials. They're also incentivized to hire the cheapest subcontractors to do the work. The cheapest people aren't necessarily the best people, so quality may be sacrificed. Because the specifications for a dental office are very exact, the subcontractors must be able to follow them precisely, but the dentist doesn't have any input or control over the hiring. Low-cost subcontractors sometimes go out of business during the course of the construction, leading to delays and unexpected costs.

Almost by definition, the relationships of team members with the hard bid approach will end up being adversarial. We don't recommend it.

In our experience, the negotiated bid approach will almost always work out to be the best option for a dental project. In a negotiated bid, the general contractor or construction manager is selected based on qualifications and experience, not just the lowest fee. The contractor's fee is negotiated in a transparent way, so everybody knows what it is.

In the negotiated bid, the general contractor is on board early in a collaborative way. Any gaps or discrepancies in the drawings are discussed and clarified before construction begins. That means change orders are rare and only happen when you truly make a change.

The subcontracted work does not necessarily go to the cheapest bidder but to the bidder who will provide the best value. The subcontractors are selected on the basis of their experience, the quality of their work, and their availability. The subcontractors are hired openly, so the design/construction team and the doctor have input. The entire process is collaborative between the contractor and the design team.

The negotiated bid approach ensures an open-book approach to pricing the project and allows flexibility if costs need to be reduced. A spirit of teamwork and cooperation governs the process. In our experience, the negotiated approach greatly increases the quality of the finished project.

The Right Team

When it comes to making the bold decision to build a new office, bringing in a management company with extensive professional design, engineering, and construction expertise is essential. To understand why, let's look at how Primus was able to help a dentist in the Midwest build the office of his dreams.

This general dentist was in his sixth year of practice. Like many young dentists, he had started out leasing an office in a small space. It wasn't ideally located, but it was within his budget. He did well despite being in a changing neighborhood. Now he was feeling established and confident of his ability to continue to grow. It was time to move on. The question he brought to us was, how?

His existing space only had three operatories. His annual collections had increased by 30 percent each year for the last three years. He was at the point where he wanted to hire an additional hygienist, but he had nowhere to put this person. His year-over-year growth and the need to bring on additional staff forced him to consider whether he should renew the lease for another five years or do something else.

As our first step, we had him complete our Vision Casting Guide. We wanted to understand his long-term goals and objectives. His answers to the Vision Casting questions told us clearly that he really saw value in owning his own building and being his own landlord. We knew from our conversations that he was both very capable and ambitious.

Renovating his current lease space was out of the question; the space couldn't possibly be redone to accommodate the eight operatories he wanted. Clearly, this dentist needed to expand, but no adjacent lease space was available. The next step was to look in his town for a new space that could be leased or an existing property that could be bought and renovated to accommodate a dental office. We ran a local search to try to find a good lease space or property. We couldn't find an appropriate lease space within his geographic area, but we did turn up an available older building that was sized appropriately. We did a tour of the building with the dentist and developed a floor plan showing how his eight operatories and other spaces could fit.

But as we worked more on the plan, the inherent limitations of that particular building became clear. It had low, eight-foot ceilings, and it turned out that the exterior would need a fair amount of repair work to bring it up to code. More importantly, based on his Vision Casting responses, this doctor really wanted an office that had a modern, contemporary look with a lot of natural light. This building was in a good location and the price was reasonable, but to turn it into what he wanted would be very costly.

No other suitable properties were available in the area. That left two options: widen the geographic area or build from the ground up. Our demographic analysis and site analysis for the area told us that moving out of the area wasn't a good option. The dentist was left with the only real choice: buy property and build a new building for the practice.

This wasn't an easy decision for our client. He was concerned about taking on so much debt and responsibility while he still had student loans to pay off. On the other hand, he felt he was up to the challenge of handling a larger practice and felt confident that his increased revenue from more patients would let him repay the money he needed to borrow. He was also very concerned about how much time a big project would take. He wanted to continue to handle his full patient load and not have to take a lot of time away from being at the chair side. He'd heard a lot of horror stories about doing a building project: slow design process, unreliable contractors, cost overruns, and huge headaches for the doctor. We explained while he would definitely need to be involved in the process to some degree, we would handle a lot of the details for him. Things like purchasing land, arranging financing, and working on the design do take time, but our job at Primus is to help the doctor through every step. Our broad experience lets us move every step forward with as little friction as possible and with as much or little involvement as a doctor wants.

Once the client decided to take the big step of building, we were able to locate three potential sites in his town that would work. Each was large enough to build a nice-sized dental office. The largest site was actually big enough to not only build a dental office but also to leave him space on the property to build another building in the future as an income property. Alternatively, he could subdivide the site and sell off the second lot, either now or down the road. The largest property was very appealing to him because one of his long-term goals was to do some property development.

Now that we had a strong candidate for the property, the time had come for our client to arrange financing. One of the financing challenges for this doctor was that his practice was still relatively new. He had started practice fresh out of school and didn't have much in the way of assets or savings. When he went to his local bank to discuss a loan, he was told the cash requirements would be high. In fact, he was told that he would need to put up between 20 and 25 percent of the total project in cash. Based on an estimated total project cost of about $1.2 million, that meant the doctor was going to have to come up with at least $240,000 in cash. He'd been aggressively paying down his student loans and reinvesting in his practice. There was no way he could come up with that amount of up-front money. The local bank was making the project very, very difficult to accomplish. Our client felt his project was dead.

Fortunately, because we've been working with dentists for years, we knew there were other, better ways to find the loan he needed. After he talked to us about his financing difficulties, we pointed out that his local bank simply didn't have enough experience with dental projects to understand that he was actually a very good credit risk. We made introductions for him to a couple of national dental specialty lenders. Because we've worked with these lenders successfully in the past, they were happy to consider our client's loan application. They had the experience and specialized knowledge to review his practice and see its trajectory of solid growth. He qualified for 100 percent financing with these lenders. With 100 percent of the financing in place, he was able to move forward.

Our next steps were to write a purchase contract for the lot, negotiate the price, and complete the purchase on behalf of the doctor.

Then the fun part started: He began the process of working with us for the site design and the design of the new office. As usual, it was a very interactive, back-and-forth process. The doctor had a specific vision of how he wanted the building to look. Our architect was able to capture that and make it work on the site. The doctor had a very particular vision for how he wanted the reception desk to look. After a couple rounds of going back and forth and exploring different options, our architect drew up the concept in a way that was exactly what the doctor had envisioned. We went through the same process for the treatment rooms to get them exactly the way he wanted them.

Once the preliminary floor plan was finalized, we brought in the dental equipment specialist the doctor was working with to further dial in the details of the treatment rooms based on the doctor's equipment selections. Next we scheduled a day for the doctor to come to our office and make all of the material and finish selections for the new office. We then moved into detailed construction documents for the entire building. We still needed some input from the doctor for these, but most of the work was engineering and infra-structure, which didn't need a lot of personal attention from him.

When the detailed construction documents were done, we took care of all the necessary permits and regulatory approvals needed from the town. As isn't uncommon with projects like this, we had to overcome a zoning problem. The zoning for the site had a requirement stating that the building had to be located immediately adjacent to the street, with the parking area behind the building. This was a challenge because it meant all of the operatories would have to face west, when facing north or east is much more desirable. We petitioned the town zoning board on the doctor's behalf. We asked for a variance that would allow us to put the parking in front of the building. That would not only allow the operatories to face the correct direction, but it also just made more sense to have the parking in the front. It made access from the street much easier because patients didn't have to drive around to the back of the building and then walk back to the street to get in.

The project was then put out for pricing using a negotiated bid approach. The pricing and contract negotiations went quickly because at Primus we have a lot of experience in this area. We know very precisely what things cost in a building project, so we're able to get fair prices and avoid expensive surprises. We also know what to look for in subcontractors, so we end up working with capable, honest people.

With everything in place to get construction started, the doctor was able to close on the loan, close on the lot, and break ground on the new building. He opened his doors on the new office about fourteen months after our first contact.

The reception area, office manager's office (back-left) and seating area of the new dental office.

He loves his new building. In his first six months there, his monthly patient count was up 35 percent. His new patient count averaged 35 percent more each month over his previous location. He's averaging about eighty new patients a month. The increased revenues mean he makes his loan payments easily each month. The most important thing to us, however, is that he has exactly the office he wants. He enjoys going to work each day in an office where everything is thoughtfully designed to meet the needs of his busy and growing practice.

We feel that the help we provided to find him a more visible location is a big reason for the increased patient count. His new office helped not just with getting new patients but also with retaining old ones.

His old leased space was a former post office that still looked a lot like a post office, just without the flagpole. Other than his small sign, there was no way to know that it was a dental office. His new building has much more curb appeal. It's an attractive, modern building with good access and good parking. Inside, the office is very spacious, especially compared to his previous waiting room, which only had space for four chairs. When patients have to stand around while they wait to see the dentist, they may get annoyed and decide to go to someone else. His new seating area has plenty of chairs and is very comfortable. By having eight up-to-date new operatories, he is able to see patients quickly instead of asking them to wait weeks or even months for an appointment. Such waits also annoy patients and make them decide to go to someone else. His patients are now sticking with him.

Because he now has the room, he has been able to hire additional hygienists to see patients. He also now has the room and patient base to start thinking about bringing in an associate dentist to accommodate the influx of patients. Most of all, he's excited to be in a space that is stylish, that's sized correctly, and that conveys who he is as a dentist and a person. He's proud of his office.

When the project was completed, he made a point of telling me two things: he is so happy he decided to build a new office, and he couldn't be happier with his decision to work with Primus. From the up-front help to the architectural design down to the construction management part, he was thrilled with how things went. He told me he couldn't have asked for a better experience—always something nice to hear!

Conclusion

A dentist spends many hours of every working day in the office. That office should be a comfortable, efficient place that meets the functional needs of your practice and aligns with your personality. When the office stops being comfortable and efficient, or starts to look outdated, it's time to consider the next steps. Renovation, expansion, moving, and building an entirely new office are all possibilities. Based on our decades of experience at Primus, we believe that whatever the choice, working with an experienced team that understands the particular needs of dentists means that an office renovation, expansion, or new build will go smoothly with little headaches, downtime, or revenue loss.

Many of the options have significant costs associated with them. For most doctors, the decision to do major renovations, move to a new space, or build their own building will be one of the biggest, if not the biggest, financial investment they make in their entire career. For this investment to pay off, it's very important to have a team of experienced people who understand you and your business behind you. We recommend working with people who have a lot of experience, not just on the design and construction end but in managing dental projects from the very beginning, when you first start to think about a new office. The decisions made at the earliest stage may have a major impact on the investment downstream.

The dentists we work with all went to school for a long time in order to become really good at one specific thing: providing excellent dental care to their patients. They're skilled at what they do because they have lots of training, both in school and on the job, and lots of experience. What they didn't learn in dental school was how to design or plan for a dental office. That's where we come in. We've worked for over twenty years to get really good at one specific thing: helping dentists achieve the office of their dreams.

At Primus, we believe that the highest and best use of a dentist's time is working in and on their practice, not working on a building project. We also believe that in today's fast-paced world, an integrated, comprehensive approach to the planning, design, and construction process for a dental project provides the most value to the dentist. It frees them to practice dentistry, spend time with their family, and do the other things in their life that matter to them.

An integrated process provides a single point of contact for every aspect of the project, as opposed to managing relationships with ten or twelve team members at various times as the project progresses. An integrated process simply makes sense. The dentist doesn't have to worry about what the civil engineer is doing, what the mechanical engineer is doing, what the interior decorator is doing, and what the contractor is doing.

We also believe that every doctor's motivations for the project are different. The objectives of one doctor—more operatories, for example—vary from another doctor, who is more concerned with moving to a more accessible location. In our experience, the reasons behind dental office projects are intensely personal. A one-size-fits-all solution isn't in the best interest of doctors. Quite the opposite, really. That is why we have developed a customized system to make growing your practice as easy and seamless as possible. The Primus Integrated Solution System is a comprehensive approach that is designed to improve project communication, anticipate potential pitfalls, prevent mistakes, and streamline completion of required project tasks. We take responsibility for executing every step of the project. Sure, it may be possible for a dentist to oversee and manage a large office project. But is that the best use of their time? Almost certainly not. Without a lot of experience in this area, the opportunities are vast for error, miscommunication, and lack of coordination.

In the end, you must be proud of your office, and it must help you achieve your personal and professional goals. The right office reduces your stress, helps you and your team be more productive, makes your patients and your staff feel comfortable and helps you enjoy coming to work each day.

If you're considering a change in your dental office for whatever reason, we are always happy to talk. For a complimentary consultation with me or one of our project consultants, please reach out to us at (877) 947-7757 or visit makingtherightimpression.com/consult. You can also visit makingtherightimpression.com for more information about the book or www.dentalbuilders.com for more informa-

tion about our company, including project photos. We look forward
to hearing from you.

About the Author

Jason Drewelow is the general manager of Primus Dental Design & Construction, a national planning, design, and construction management firm established in Cedar Rapids, Iowa. Primus specializes in dental and medical office facilities. Jason is an expert at working with dentists and dental specialists, helping them to create offices that improve practice efficiencies, increase production, and reflect the distinct personalities of the owner-dentist.

Primus Dental Design & Construction has completed more than four hundred dental office projects nationwide since 1995. They understand the complexity that goes into building or renovating a dental office. Primus partners with their clients at every step of the planning, architectural design, interior design, and construction stages of a project. They do it all, from securing a location, to meeting regulatory requirements, to designing an efficient office layout, to hiring trades people and supervising the construction from start to finish.

Because Primus provides property selection, architecture, interior design, and construction management services all in one company, dentists who work with us can continue to be dentists while we work on their new offices. Our integrated approach saves them time and money and helps to limit the hours spent away from their practice. Pulling from our extensive network within the dental community, Primus can also help with financing, IT, and consulting partners that will help guarantee the success of your project.

When Jason Drewelow isn't at work, he enjoys being with his family. He spends much of his time coaching his sons' sports teams or snowboarding. Among his other interests are reading, hiking, biking, and watching the Indianapolis Colts, the Chicago Cubs, and the Iowa Hawkeyes.

CPSIA information can be obtained
at www.ICGtesting.com
Printed in the USA
LVHW070340080819
626896LV00004B/6/P